D0986905

# MARINE LOVER

Luce Irigaray

# MARINE LOVER
## OF FRIEDRICH NIETZSCHE

TRANSLATED BY GILLIAN C. GILL

Columbia University Press
NEW YORK

BOWLING GREEN STATE
UNIVERSITY LIBRARIES

Columbia University Press wishes to express its appreciation of assistance given by the government of France through Le Ministère de la Culture in the preparation of this translation.

Columbia University Press
New York    Oxford
*Amante marine* copyright © Les Editions de Minuit
Copyright © 1991 Columbia University Press
All rights reserved
Casebound editions of Columbia University Press books are Smyth-sewn and printed on permanent and durable acid-free paper

Printed in the United States of America

c 10 9 8 7 6 5 4 3 2 1

Library of Congress Cataloging-in-Publication Data

Irigaray, Luce.
    [Amante marine. English]
    Marine lover of Friedrich Nietzsche / Luce Irigaray
    : translated by Gillian C. Gill.
    p.   cm.—
    Translation of: Amante marine.
    ISBN 0–231–07082–9
    1. Nietzsche, Friedrich Wilhelm, 1844–
    1900.   I. Title.
B3317.I7413   1991
193—dc20                                    90-27059
                                                CIP

# CONTENTS

# MARINE LOVER

# SPEAKING
# OF IMMEMORIAL WATERS

## BAPTISM OF THE SHADOW

And you had all to lose sight of me so I could come back, toward you, with an other gaze.

And, certainly, the most arduous thing has been to seal my lips, out of love. To close off this mouth that always sought to flow free.

But, had I never held back, never would you have remembered that something exists which has a language other than your own. That, from her prison, someone was calling out to return to the air. That your words reasoned all the better because within them a voice was captive. Amplifying your speech with an endless resonance.

I was your resonance.

Drum. I was merely the drum in your own ear sending back to itself its own truth.

And, to do that, I had to be intact. I had to be supple and stretched, to fit the texture of your words. My body aroused only by the sound of your bell.

Today I was this woman, tomorrow that one. But never the woman, who, at the echo, holds herself back. Never the beyond you are listening to right now.

Yes, yes, yes . . . I hear you. And I do not hear you. I am your hearing. Between you and yourself, I ensure the vocal medium. A perpetual relay between your mouth and your ear. Go on, I am singing your memory so that you do not fall into some abyss of forgetfulness.

How I should love you if to speak to you were possible.

And yet I still love you too well in my silence to remember the movement of my own becoming. Perpetually am I troubled, stirred, frozen, or smothered by the noise of your death.

The recollection of my birth still lies stifled under the din of your hate. Or the shroud of your indifference.

For, round and round, you keep on turning. Within yourself. Pushing out of your circle anything that, from elsewhere, remembers.

But I am coming back from far, far away. And say to you: your horizon has limits. Holes even.

You have always trapped me in your web and, if I no longer serve as your passage from back to front, from front to back, your time will let an other day dawn. Your world will unravel. It will flood out to other places. To that outside you have not wanted.

☆

Yes, I am coming back from far, far away. And my crime, at present, is my candor.

I am no longer the lining to your coat, your—faithful—understudy. Voicing your joys and sorrows, your fears and resentments. You had fashioned me into a mirror but I have dipped that mirror in the waters of oblivion—that you call life. And farther away than the place where you are beginning to be, I have turned back. I have washed off your masks and make up, scrubbed away your multicolored projections and designs, stripped off your veils and wraps that hid the shame of your nudity. I have even had to scrape my woman's flesh clean of the insignia and marks you had etched upon it.

That was the most painful hour. For you had so deeply implanted these things into me that almost nothing was left to recall me to the innocence of my life. Almost nothing to let me rediscover my own becoming beyond your sufferings. All that was left—barely—was a breath, a hint of air and blood that said: I want to live. And why should living always be misfortune? And why should I always be security for your misery? The test of your bad luck? If you care nothing for living, then death will be for you a surer place of eternal peace.

As for me, your death seems too base and miserly to satisfy my mobility. Your calculations and half-measures and half-shades make everything into little enclosures where anyone ceaselessly restless constantly bangs into the fence. My whole body is divided up into neatly ruled sections. Each of them allotted to one private owner or

4

another. Which belongs to whom?—shrieks such and such a part. And no one replied, for each man claimed the whole. If his whole comes to seem merely a part, then he no longer recognizes it and prefers to give up the whole so he can keep his dream safe and sound.

Since no one was answering "me," I felt free of obligation to anyone and found myself alone in strange country.

The whole was immense, and I knew that I should never fail to be able to go farther on. I had been taught that a woman who belonged to no one was nothing, and I laughed, I really laughed to hear such startling news. How surprising that I had believed them for so long.

Nothing? This whole that always and at every moment was thus becoming new? Nothing? This endless coming into life at each moment? Nothing? This whole that had laid by the mantle of long sleep and was reviving all my senses? Nothing, this unfathomable well?

How could they have been so wrong? Was it deliberate? Absolutely? Only half? Why? And would the gold of their setting sun help me find the strength to say to them: here is the future, in that past that you never wanted. If I melt their gold into light, might they then open their eyes to see a new day dawning?

How to get them beyond their love of gold? To get them to see beyond gold? Is life ever given in exchange for gold? And if indeed one must dig the land in order to put down roots, if a man persists in changing into gold the lode that he finds, is it not death that he worships?

And when I had laughed at your weapons of death, then (I) came out of the earth, and my eyes lit up.

Different bodies, that no doubt makes the likeness. For, in the other, how is one to find oneself except by also throwing one's self-same (son même) there? And, between you (tu)* and me, will there not always be this film that keeps up apart?

If you were to gaze on yourself in me, and if in you also I could find my reflection, then those dreams would unlimit our spaces. But

---

*At this point the speaking subject addresses a masculine "tu" as opposed to the masculine "vous" of the opening section.—Tr.

5

if I keep your images and you refuse to give me back mine, your self-same (ton même) is but a prison. Love of you but a paralysis. The moving universe of our entwining mirages becomes the mirroring outline of your world. The mists rising from our encounters become a cloud blotting out the sun, blocking off the horizon.

The sun? What sun? And why should it hide the sun from us unless it is the same sun that you have taken over as the projector of your circle?

But this torch, your lamp, makes shadow. Even (même) at noon. Even/self (même) seeing itself. Your noon leaves in the darkness the other side of the earth, and its inside, and the depths of the sea.

Does your noon itself not have an other side? Do you see behind your sun? What does your sun illumine that is added or taken away from the fullness of your hour?

And are there no other stars more brilliant than a sun? Where are those fires burning at the time of your highest light?

And why weariness and sorrow at the most perfect hour of your day? Whence comes the evil that you should fret over past or future? So bitter and hesitant, despite the wonders you flaunt. As you steady yourself and hang on tightly to the shore to be sure of a peaceful haven.

Might your hour be only that of sleep? Might you have been gone too long to want anything but to nod off at high noon?* Eyes open, and the soul alert.

But the soul is long and weary, as on the evening of a seventh day. Stretched thin and forced to stretch out thinner yet over her ages, and now anxious simply to melt into the shadow of the silence of the earth.

Lips closed but puckered as of one who doesn't yet know if he still can wish, who is still hanging on by some thread to his old anchorage.

An old noon your hour is, and the sun has to give his all for a single drop to be drunk from it. From so high and so far and with

---

*In translating this passage I have relied in some measure on Walter Kaufman's rendering of the "At Noon" section of *Thus Spoke Zarathustra*, pp. 387–390 in *The Portable Nietzsche* (Penguin Books, 1954).—Tr.

such force must he beat down if the taste of a single moment is again to be savored. Quite separate from the feasts and plenty of old.

For the taste is spoiled by an excess of good things. Little is enough to one who knows how to live. The smallest of trifles is surely wealth to one learning not to love gold. Surely the lightest, liveliest caress means more than thick layers of hoarded possessions. Is this not so?

But to help you make such finds you have only the breath of air still allowed at the fullness of noon. That still touches you and makes you shiver in the still circle of the height of your day. That perfect round you stand in. Were it not for that invisible breeze that still moves in and around your heavy noon, who would pull you out of your deep, deep dreams? From your well of eternity?

Only a breath of wind needs to stir and your perfection is ready to vanish. Such is your highest hour.

And are your legs not too old now to run after perfection? Too weak to chase her down? Which way?

If your heart is broken, is it not better for you to go back to sleep than dare to wake up? In order to live that half of eternity still left you.

Yes, of course, better the whole than the half. And better to give your soul back to the abyss of noon than to share your hour, if she can gulp you down into her eternity.

But how to turn back, and as a (female) whole, into that from which one comes? For either your soul loses its wondrous roundness, or the place of turning back is merely a bottomless well.

You fold the membrane between us in your own way. Either it is right side up and thrust out, or turned faltering back into yourself. For holes mean only the abyss to you. And the further out you project yourself, the farther you fall. There is nothing to stop your penetration outside yourself—nothing either more or less. Unless I am there.

The membrane was not yours to have. We formed it together. And if you want it for yourself, you make a hole in it just because I lack any part. And don't you make God out of that absence?

But if your God dies, how keen is your distress. Endless is your despair and your rage to destroy even the very beginning of this nothingness. The more you seek out the source of danger and strive to control it, the more abyssal is the tomb. Before, when you gazed at the stars, at least you left earth the chance of her secret. Now you dig down into the earth to recover something she has taken or withheld from you. But nothing is hidden from you by this ground that keeps your footsteps.


BEYOND MID-NIGHT

And if a single day, a single feast, satisfies you (vous) for not having lived your life? If an encounter, one day, with a single man comforts you for having in death placed your time. On the earth, with no love of the earth. If the unique question of a master, divine to be sure, brings about such a change, such a healing in you that, given this one gift, you cast weariness aside—then if the dance is yours, oh higher men, or the dance of the ass, what does it matter!*

And from your thankless thanks, from your laughter and tears, from your caresses and embraces, will steal away anyone who still desires to walk toward the star. From your rites, from your raptures, your drunken passion, (he) turns swiftly away, and bids you be silent, to listen further. To leave your day so that you can move out into the night.

For you are barely beginning to savor the sweet life when mid-night overtakes you late-comers. Who always made a curse of darkness. Failing to taste the thought of the night, you remained ever in shadow.

And now your sun is in the setting, and you are summoned to the memory of mid-night, you last-minute seekers. The irony of your time condemns you to open your eyes on what has already gone by, only after your knell has rung. Just as you emerge from oblivion, oblivion swallows you up. For always (you) arrive too late at the moment of living.

"Was *that* life?"† Perhaps. But here is death. And your conversion takes place only when the turn of your wheel is over. Only when,

---

*"Higher men" is the expression Walter Kaufman chooses for *Zarathustra*, book 4, where the higher men congregated in Zarathustra's mountain cave have an ass festival.—Tr.

†" 'My friends, all of you,' said the ugliest man, what do you think? For the sake of this

faced with what you have always wanted, you now want—the opposite. That is your fortune!

But since you still have a little time left, and you can no longer stay on at the feast, listen, at least this once, to what your mid-night has to say. The man who leads you into rapture, he at least knows what the night brings. That the (female) one without the other can neither be given nor received—this he knows who has woken up a little earlier than you have. That the (female) one without the other cannot be willed—this he already knows who has outlived his age. And that your raptures taste of death because you refuse to taste death—this he already knows who beyond your life and your death pursues his way.

He brings you back to the one who has lived more experiences than any single man. She who counted one by one the beatings of your hearts, and your fathers' hearts. And who from suffering, sighs, and laughs. The old, deep mid-night to whom one may not speak aloud in the daytime. And whose many voices rise up when the tumult of your hearts is still.

And thus the unheard speaks to you, and slips into your nocturnal soul which, this once, is not sleeping. And says: "Oh man! take care."

Take care that time does not fly by and you (tu) are not already dead. That you have not sunk into bottomless wells through turning a deaf ear to the thought of mid-night.

And your last dream is that some spider weaving her web around you is after your blood. For you are caught in her web. And no spider exists but the one you wove to make your circle. And yet you drew the stuff of your web from the womb of a (female) other, did you not?

And this is what love is for you—wanting to give your blood when everything is over.

If the hour of ice and frost rings out for you, can you answer for your heart in that ordeal? If mastery of the earth is to fall to him

---

day, *I* am for the first time satisfied that I have lived my whole life. And that I attest so much is still not enough for me. Living on earth is worth while: one day, one festival with Zarathustra, taught me to love the earth. 'Was *that* life?' I want to say to death. 'Well then! Once more!' " (*Zarathustra*, p. 429).—Tr.

who no longer belongs to the earth, isn't it likely you will just go back to your tomb-robbing instead of rising up to such a height?

But will those corpses do you any good? Surely it is already too late, oh higher man, for you to become an earthworm. For you will have to dig down deep, much deeper than your day ever imagined, to bring the dead back to life.

But he, that man soaring high, and who has already given up the use of his legs and the dances of a man in favor of wings, he hears another toll of the bell. Wild, far distant lyre from the pools of love reaches his ear. Out of the depths it comes, from beneath the tombs, and high it soars. And anyone deaf to such extremes will never hear that song, only mutterings from the graves.

But the man who heeds that music through the air, what does he want? To die. To die again, that is his fortune. For at mid-night (he) has found a death more intoxicating in its depths than the death of his day. And in this song, which from afar is recalled, (he) hears nothing but the accomplishment of his hour. And (he) smells nothing but the perfume of eternity in that scent rising up from before the beginning of his death.

Thus he wishes to receive only what beats in time to the rhythm he sets. And nothing is in store for him at mid-night except what, at his midday, he stored away. And if mid-night be even darker than his day had imagined, that is the way his star still rises to perfect his circle.

And if for you pleasure is the return of the same, and if everything returns "one more time," that is to say "for ever and ever." And if nothing is thus lost of either the highest dream or the sharpest pain. If you insist on love and hate remaining caught up in one another so that one never occurs without the other. If your pleasure can never untangle itself from suffering, and the most extreme advance of your genius is to go deep into the deepest depths of the flesh, since that bite stirs your vigilance at the hour of mid-night, then, indeed, let me go out of your shadow.

For night, to me, is not that. And there is no need for you to perfect your day by dragging me from slumber. For sleep, to me, is no disappearance. And for each hour, its own fortune suffices. And it pleases me not that the hours should repeat themselves and fade one into the other according to the orb of your single sun—that your will should always be at least twice times one, and the same again. So that this way everything happens and happens to be what you are. That, for your eternity, everything should always turn in a circle, and that within that ring I should remain—your booty.

For every hour, in its firstness, its uniqueness, pleases me.

And when everything starts again, already (I) am gone elsewhere. Whole (I) shall be at every moment, and every whole moment. And he who repeats so that time will come back has already separated himself from time.

But to each second you say: I've got you. And already (that second/elle) is gone while you were watching. And you with it. When your last hour tolls, it will still find you holding back the first from running away. And none of them will you have lived, since you never stayed in its element.

Everything turns, and turns back and around, no doubt. But not inside you. What are you using as a pivot for everything so that you can tie up the two ends? That your will forms the axis, I realize of course. But if I take leave of your universe, what becomes of it?

And since I have never mellowed, and since my time has not yet come, I still want to live.

And if your hour ends when mine beings, that gives me no pleasure. For I love to share, whereas you want to keep everything for yourself.

But musing over the pain of that final reckoning is no reck of mine. Better far the pleasure of walking, hour by hour, toward a new dawn.

Let me go. Yes, let me go onward. Beyond the place of no return. Either you seize hold of me or you throw me away, but always according to your whim of the moment. I am good or bad according to your latest good or evil. Muse or fallen angel to suit the needs of your most recent notion.

And heaven or earth, rock or air, foothold or abyss, midday or midnight, according to the day that tolls for you. And I am broken by all these to-ings and fro-ings. As weary of hope as of despair—since both amount to the same.

Are you waiting for me to scream out so loudly in distress that the wall of your deafness is broken down? For me to call you out farther than the farthest recesses you frequent? Out of your circle?

But isn't that your game: ceaselessly to bring the outside inward? To have no outside that you have not put there yourself? My scream would then be merely the sign of your recall.

But (I) no longer wish to return into you. As soon as I am inside, you will vomit me up again. And I should prefer to explore the bottom of the sea than make these journeys into and out of your present.

Too long have I been held back by the thread of compassion. I wanted a better destiny for you—and me. How is it possible, from the weight of his destiny, to unburden the man who submits to it?

Moving on is surely the road to take when love takes such a road. And surely this farewell is the sign of love. Opening your horizon again to a more distant coming.

## RAPTURE OF INCORRUPTIBLE SEA

Into the sea (you) are returned, to live your loneliness. And ten years, without weariness, you took pleasure (jouis) in your spirit. The sea used to carry you, but in no way troubled your fortune. You sought to become a child again, to climb ashore and drag your man's body once more.*

Why leave the sea? To carry a gift—of life. But it is to the earth that you preach fidelity. And forgetfulness of your birth. Not knowing if you descend from a monkey or a worm or if you might even be some cross between plant and ghost.†

Anxious to resolve this discord, you teach the superman: the

---

*Again I am indebted to Walter Kaufman's translation of the Prologue to *Thus Spoke Zarathustra*. After ten years in the mountains, Zarathustra announces to the sun that he "must descend to the depths." An old man says to him, "Zarathustra has changed. Zarathustra has become a child. Zarathustra is an awakened one; what do you now want among the sleepers? You lived in your solitude, as in the sea, and the sea carried you. Alas, would you now climb ashore? Alas, would you again drag your own body?" (*The Portable Nietzsche*, pp. 122–123).—Tr.

† See Kaufman, *The Portable Nietzsche*, p. 125.—Tr.

meaning of the earth. But do you come from earth or sea to announce this news? Is it fluid depths or solid volume that engendered you?

Are you fish or eagle, swimmer or dancer, when you announce the decline of man? Do you seek to sink or climb? Flow out or fly up? And in your entire will for the sea are you so very afraid that you must always stay up so high?

Perched on any mountain peak, hermit, tightrope walker or bird, you never dwell in the great depths. And as companion you never choose a sea creature. Camel, snake, lion, eagle, and doves, monkey and ass, and... Yes. But no to anything that moves in the water. Why this persistent wish for legs, or wings? And never gills?

And when you say that the superman is the sea in whom your contempt is lost, that's fine. That is a will wider than man's own. But you never say: the superman has lived in the sea. That is how he survives.

It is always hot, dry, and hard in your world. And to excel for you always requires a bridge.

Are you truly afraid of falling back into man? Or into the sea?

☆

Yet is there any greater rapture than the sea? For he who climbs high to set his senses areel as if from good wine must still climb down again at last. And his rapture lasts only so long. And all kinds of depressions lie in wait, and the spell is often broken.

But endless rapture awaits whoever trusts the sea. For as she rises and falls, so one's rapture swells and sinks. Whether the sea is rising or falling, nothing changes in the enchantment of living— moving about endlessly. And does it matter if the sea is pouring over the beaches or sinking back into its bed? Doesn't the one will the other, and the other the one? And isn't it the passage from one to the other that makes for eternal good fortune?

And what presumption is this to claim that you raise all the deep seas up to your heights? Did you ever reach their heights? And when you aver that the seas wish to become mountain tops and light, isn't this the talk of a man of ressentiment* who says, "As long as the sea remains sea, some movement resists my will. Some path of light is hidden from me in the sea."

And if the sun, in the innocent and impatient ardor of his rising, comes first to the sea to drink, why interpret this as the sea's will to become air so that she can rise up after him?

☆

Do you prefer to spill over or to taste your depths? When you soar highest, where do you go?

What do you want, old man? To remove me from my fortune? Because both flowing over my banks and savoring my great depths are equal rapture for me. I do not wish to be measured out drop by drop. Drop by drop (I) do not care to live my time. For whole and entire (I) want myself at every instant.

And what matter if it be ebb or flow? As long as, at each moment, (I) move as a whole. And, for me, ebb and flow have always set the rhythm of time. But (they) come at different hours. At midday or midnight, at dawn or dusk. One moment is worth absolutely no more than the other, for the whole is present in each. At each hour comes fortune, multiple in the unwinding of its becoming.

And (I) have no need to turn round and round to come back to the same or to enter into eternity.

For same have (I) been from all eternity, and, at the same time, ever different. And thus (I) come and go, change and stay, go on and come back, without any circle. Spread out and open in this endless becoming.

And without one direction ever being more important than another, without my ever wanting one rather than the other. For they are not distinct. Which is not to say that they are indistinguishable.

And (I) rise and ebb twice every day. (I) have two middays and two midnights during the time your sun takes to complete his circuit. Twice (I) get up and go to bed, while he follows his course on the near side and on the far side of your earth.

And could it be because he hides from you half the time that you

---

*Nietzsche uses the French word "ressentiment" in his text and I have retained it in English. The excellent newer translation of Nietzsche by Golfing renders "ressentiment" as "rancor."—Tr.

run after him all the time this way? Because at times he shows himself to you and at other times to others that you want to keep hold of this star and prevent him from appearing where you are not? Wanting to find the sun again at mid-night, doesn't that amount to wanting to steal the other man's midday from him? The refusal to savor night and repose—from heat, light, and drought—because at this hour the other is living his highest fortune?

Isn't your sun-worship also a kind of ressentiment? Don't you measure your ecstasy against the yardstick of envy? And isn't your circle made of the will to live this irradiation—there will be no other but me?

☆

But what in this perfection have you forgotten of yourself? What in this kingdom have you curbed of yourself? What remains of yourself in the shadow where you abandoned the other?

If wanting ever higher means taking fortune from the other, your excelling leads to greater ressentiment—still (you) have not yet overcome the other.

The inability to floor the other completely is your limit today. And the inability to savor the happiness of others as greater rapture is your evil. To share the life of the other without stealing the other's goods is a threshold you refuse to cross. A circle you will not break. A skin you will not shed.

And when you claim to digest the whole in your stomach, is it not here that your sickness lies? And the poison for your body? And the potion conjuring up phantoms? And the pledge of being ventriloquial? And of sending things back in the form of celestial nothingness.

Within you, something of the other becomes nothing—resists absorption. And something becomes death—the difference of the bodies that you claim in this way to overcome.

## WHERE YOUR BODY BEGINS AND WHERE IT ENDS

And why should innocence imply forgetfulness and beginning again? Why should the first movement be turning around in a circle? What is the one spinning eternally around saying "yes" to? To his

15

self/same. His child, for example. This same that he has always wished to become. And he will have no other child. The measurement of his world, for example. And the freedom of his creation— that everything turns around him and nothing moves except by him and according to his strength.

And the strength to say "yes" to oneself is certainly not nothing. But if in this sense everything turns and turns back and again, surely this is a sign of turning in the void, when nothing comes from the other to keep the movement going?

And does childhood have no duty other than to go back to the childhood of its fathers, in order to overcome? Could one not break the spell of that circle by saying: yes? And do I care for the before or the after if, in this moment, I become, were it only for that morning hour—the innocence of a will that is still free of the burden of a memory. Of a: you must overcome.

To weigh down a child's step with the burden of history when he barely recalls where his ball came from, and when, before playing, he has still to be able to call the ball back, is this not the dream of a God?

That is not the first duty of a child, who should rather run after his mother, and away from her, and back again, weaving threads so that his world keeps hold of that creative female presence.

And if such innocent pleasure is taken away by the will of the man and again of the superman, what becomes of the child's games? Only a drunkard who has lost the road home, and forgotten the taste of good wine. Drunk from spinning round in gaudy rags that cling to no flesh.

"I want," says childhood? No doubt. But why only to turn cartwheels? And around what is the child moving? And what is innocence enclosing in this circle? Chimaeras of back-worlds are already at work, are they not, when one yields to ressentiment on the first day?

It is a dream to want childhood to be already inspired by the highest will. And that, to distract a divinely dissatisfied being from suffering, would keep his eyes fixed on a perfect movement.

It is delirium to imagine childhood as an eternal hoop. To spin around, there must still be an axis, still in the center. And anyone coming into the world for the first time never stays still.

16

These are the visions of childhood ghosts and of specters who retrace their steps, pulled back to the point where they are tied down. And they already turn around death, do they not? Already they are anchored to death. In death they return to the same.

The childhood (f.) that knows neither "I" nor "you" prefers to go its way without turning back. It projects into the other and receives the other into herself without the one ever becoming separate from the other. Without the other being preferable to the one.

And endlessly goes and comes into the one and into the other. And nothing is the same for such as her but the refusal to return to the same.

For where is she at any one moment? Where is the limit between self and other? Where is the world? And the circle traced? Never where it might be expected.

Never death where one might have expected death—in a place where it might have been circumvented. Everywhere and nowhere. And before you can put death outside, you must first catch it. And if death is always between, nothing but a passage, then death is neither before nor after.

He who wishes to master death spends his time jumping endlessly further out. But he gives death all his time and never catches anything. He can go all round the world jumping in circles, still he will have gone past nothing. Not even his dream.

And between himself and the other, he will have created only a void. Surely, he will need to jump higher and higher, and round and round his world, or else tumble into that abyss.

Of the other, he will retain only the necessity to keep himself in a tight circle so as not to plunge downward. Only the memory of fear, the feeling of falling, the vision of hell, that comes from avoiding the passage between. From jumping over, instead of letting the feet go where they would.

Nothing of the other is retained but the footstep, and the hole that opens up beneath the feet. This is the fortune of the superman— those footsteps that circle endlessly round and round the same radii of a circle and thus keep their balance even on the dizzying edge.

All that remains of the other is a taut rope that plays with the

17

void by keeping it always at an even distance. There is no other but the axle that allows an infinite series of cartwheels, a dizzy rapture every moment that never loses its spell.

Unless the other says: I want to become outside of your world. The time is past when I stayed still to enable you to keep moving. What do I care about sharing in your games! If, by doing so, I must give up my own.

Between "I" and "you," I want there to be once again a passage and a sharing in life and in death. And not stay you within you. To make you even more I—jumping higher, spinning faster, living without living, and being satisfied when you soar high above.

Overcome, overpower, overman, isn't this flying over life? Life is what matters to me, not the beyond that snatches food from the man still struggling to live. He who needs to drink the blood of earthly creatures does not fly on his own wings. He is merely a rapacious specter beating back the depths of the air with his dreams.

And you will pitch yourself to a higher creation not by devouring the other so it is reduced to your own substance, but rather by letting different bodies be and their fortune multiply.

☆

For take care, o man: he who drinks another's blood drinks a magic potion. Greatness that feeds in that way runs risk of greater sickness. To live on the body of the other, to slip in furtively to drain the sap, and make believe that one has found new fortune within the self, such indeed are the resources of dead gods.

It within yourself you no longer find the strength to live, might it not be time to listen to the other, rather than tear holes in her body and drain her blood drop by drop? It is voices from beyond the grave who take such food, is it not? Messengers of death who drink such wine?

And in order to speak the meaning of the earth, is it necessary to exhaust all her stores? Is the reign of the superman at hand when the whole of the earth becomes sublime discourse, when all that remains of her is her praise in the memory of ghosts?

If to be body whole and entire and nothing else means also taking the other's body, then keep your soul, old man! Go on playing with your reason, your mind, your beliefs. There is relative peace on the earth when you keep busy with things other than bodies. For, whenever that question, "Where is my body?" is reborn in you, what do you do but go right back to digging in the earth who has always kept it for you.

And are you not prepared even to steal from her the song she might sing of that memory? Will you relieve her of a burden or scratch away all her living layers? And how will you know the difference if, in your soul, the limits of your body disappear?

When you say: "This is my body," how is this ultimate thought fomented? How does it happen that today pleasure and suffering are values on a par with your will? How do you come to imagine this new fervor? Who whispers to you to feel sorrow and joy in your last day?

And is it too late for you to do that? Haven't you spent your life despising what you now want most?

And don't you remember with ressentiment what you might have felt when your time came? What your passions were? Refusing to acknowledge your unhappiness, except in distant outline, your cry now is: "Let everything perish!" And your game—to drag everything down with you.

Thus you spend your final hour—trying to destroy what you have never succeeded in living. And the rage of your contempt matches your greed.

But since I have never mellowed, I still want to live. And if your hour ends when mine begins, that gives me no pleasure. For I love to share whereas you want to keep everything for yourself.

☆

Obviously, wanting to share means pain for me. But if here and now I give everything I discover, doesn't this deprive the other of his safeguard? Force him beyond his clothing of the moment? Oblige him to enter into his nudity?

By wishing to favor him thus with his highest fortune, don't I really visit suffering, shame, and disgust upon him? For to man who

19

has always conceived strength and rapture in terms of weapons and insignia, is it not death to speak to him beyond those deathly toys?

And if my deepest inspiration has come to me from a god, to whom may I offer it today without its poisoning him? If for men their God is dead, where can the divine be spoken without preaching death? Where can the music be sung that calls neither to the unique nor to the eternal but to this new tiding—there is no greater happiness than living, no greater rapture than love.

And if I only love you naked and without adornment, will this love today be lovable for you? Does this lofty adventure that needs no warmer wrapping than your skin mean nothing to you but a fall from your highest heights? Does it mean tearing those dearly won shrouds of glory away from you rag by rag when I say: now begin again, you have yet to begin to live.

(We) have still not begun to live, (you) fall back short. Learn what was the foundation of everything you have built up. If you want to rise up once more, remember the earth you take flight from. For if she were to fail you, you would lose the very sensation of height.

Deeper than the solid crust you must now descend to announce the meaning of the earth. Remember what happens on the inside so that you can be sure of where you are running on the outside. And realize that a solid plane is never just a solid plane. That it rests on subterranean and submarine life, on capped fires and winds which yet stir ceaselessly beneath that shell.

## THE BURDEN OF THE PEAKS

And when you move from peak to peak, do you use a pole to vault away from death, or springs snatched from whatever it is that struggles to live beneath your skin? Do your flight, your laughter, and your fits of rage come from your blood, or are they nothing but the tricks of a man already dead and whom nothing can stop since he has no place anymore in his body? Ghost, tightrope walker, or overfed dreamer, is that your superman? Or the man who too long has curbed his yearning flesh within a tomb?

Does your cycle mimic the circulation of your blood? Or else the circling pilgrimage, at an equal distance from his origin, of one who always scorns even to remember what sustains him as he goes? Are you at last a living being or still a puppet tied tighter than ever to its destiny?

Yes, my fortune would be to rediscover your limit. And, coming closer to the boundaries of your body, to journey back to the wellspring of your life with you, allowing you also to sip from mine. And to join those first springs which have been dammed up beneath appearances and waste of all kinds.

Arrive at your skin and say to you: come back this way once more, and heedless of the membrane enveloping us, let us embrace once more. And instead of a tearing, let it be a return to something that has never taken place. The embrace of earth and air and fire and water, which have never been wed. Forget the knife-cuts, the chalk-line partitions. Forget the appropriations at frontiers that belong to no one and are marked by arbitrarily solid lines that risk the abyss at every moment. The forfeit of the will, the insecurity of the debt, the death of the gods, the end of being. Speech stealing into ghosts or clockwork dolls who have only the mouths still left them by the living.

Isn't it time to melt down the idols and to prevent others, of even less value, being fashioned from the metal? Idols even more fascinating because they are the work of artists more and more gifted in lies. Of dreamers drifting further and further away from any imitation of nature. Rapture more and more rapt in overcoming life.

And if your imagination unfolds through analogies based on your single and unique world, where can your dreams spill over? So far into appearance that nothing remains to be given contours, and colors, and meaning. A universe now so ethereal that there is no stuff to make a work of art.

Yes of course, you are perched up very high now. But can any sap reach you? Isn't your tree held up by the stalk of a stalk? The line of a line, the drawing of a drawing, the sketch of a sketch of the past still remembered in the eye of your mind? And gray monochrome serves for living colors as you write there, up on your perch.

And when you have endlessly traced the circle of your story in black on black, where will you go then? Won't you have wiped out even your footprints? O, you late-comer, as you soar away, covering your tracks by one last repetition, won't you have thrown into the chasm of an imperceptible illusion that body that, at the last, you wanted to save?

☆

But what do (you) care about what is over and done with, since (you) have already gone off in search of other mirages and won't have to put up with such sights. And if you still come back to drink a little blood at night, daylight won't find you killing, but flying.

Far over your crimes you soar, you the superman. And make tragedies merely into an occasional floor to dance on.

"Murderer, me? All I wanted to do was fly." –"So you killed so that you could fly?" –"What do you mean by that? Because if you think flying brought me to crime, you're making a mistake. And if you judge that I have been able to fly because I profited by the murder I did, you're wrong again. I was flying at the same time as I was killing. My crime is my flight or my flight is my crime." –"Those two acts cannot be carried out at the same time." –"Yet that is my truth. Doesn't it fall within the jurisdiction of your courts? How do you judge a man whose flight and crime are one and the same, and the one cannot be distinguished from or identified with the other? Do you have a legal code that allows such a feat to be condemned? And how do you punish the man who confounds the counts of your indictment?"

Leaving your judges weary and tearing each other apart with their arguments, you laugh at the self-evidence of your truth, and fly away again.

That is the mark of your genius: you strike blows that land and fade in seemingly free air. You pass through all laws, since your good and your evil are still not written up in books. And even horror remains legitimate as long as good folk refuse to see it. And look away from such sights. Veil themselves in a justice that is too honest for rascals of your sort.

For don't your freedom and your healing originate in your crimes, which let you spring up higher into flight? Farther and farther away from the courts of good folks? Once you were prisoner and patient, walled up by your faults and suffering from doubt, but now you rave on with impunity.

By certifying you as mad, are they not confirmed in their wisdom? And who could convict a madman? Has he not placed himself beyond all judgment? Through the holes in such nets he slips. And anyone who tries to stop him is soon raving too.

But the truth that you are really mad has yet to be proven. And what does it matter! Let your destiny decide. And the future of your decline.

And the more you aim for height and light, the more powerfully you are rooted in evil. That is how your world was built—the good in it always assumes the evil. Whoever rises up turns away from and towards evil. And there is no end to that infernal coupling.

Each step up can be measured by the crime following in its wake. And the more you thirst after the stars, the more your wild dogs howl after the cruelest of pleasures.

Such is the purity of your love. This is what it keeps of age-old destruction. Of insolence and ridicule at the highest hour. For will the hope that hour heralds outlast a thunder bolt? The lightning rips high through the sky indeed. And heroic is its messenger—until your wings are burned off.

And how to live that second that refutes the first? Hoping and despairing endlessly. And never wearying of those blows that land over and over again and on which you build your unique love and your only woman: eternity.

But if your only love is for eternity, why stay on this earth? If pleasures and mortifications, for you, are perpetually bound together, why don't you give up living? If birth amounts to a beginning of death, why drag out the agony?

Could it be that your nostalgia lacks the strength needed for so glorious a destiny? "Heavy is life," you go around telling anyone willing to listen. When is this melancholy old refrain going to end? If the taste of eternal life eternally haunts you, why prolong this passage through death?

Waiting is weariness and you lack the assurance to do it pleasurably. And whereas I pity your patience, (I) have no desire to encourage it. For your sermons on death are wearisome and my ears favor music other than funeral eulogies.

☆

If I didn't have to carry your burdens, I should walk more lightly toward my time. And if I didn't have to bear your ills, how I should dance!

But (she) who keeps to the dark, the deep, and the heavy, must of course lie prostrate all through your day. Isn't just staying on top of the ground and not letting yourself (vous) get buried already enough of a job when all the world's fatality falls to your lot? When, from midnight to the highest hour, the darkness of memory devolves upon you? When, in the density of your flesh, the superman's flight takes root?

And, should you stir even ever so slightly, that tightrope walker up there may fall into the abyss! That is how he manages to stay up there alone—if you don't remain the prisoner of his lack of freedom, he falls! And as (he) takes each next step, (he) suffers from the risk that it entails! And each time (he) plunges back into the depths of the flesh, her stillness exalts him and (he) thrills at the brilliance of his new exploit! As with her subterranean and submarine strength she keeps the rope secure for his glorious ascent.

And she urges him to go up again, so as to feel the pain even more sharply.

## CONTEMPT FOR YOUR NOSTALGIA

And it would suit me better to appear as your worst enemy than that you (tu) should pretend to spare me. For what does such restraint mean? This caution in warfare?

If deep down you really loved me, wouldn't you accept the truth? In your heart lurks envy, that, out of shame, you still won't expose to the light of day.

But your eyes will not be free of hate until your sun lights up the darkness of your soul. Night will always blur your sight as long as you show me nothing but a good heart. Behind you trails she whom you will not see. At your back crawls, polluting the landscape, she whom you will not fight out in the open. That shadow who separates us and whom you refuse to look straight in the eye for a fight to the bitter end.

How can one attack such a pretty engaging little girl, your spite whispers in your ear. And whom are you talking about? Who is this girl who lacks courage? Are you, perhaps, such a coward that you cover your retreat under a popinjay's arrogance?

A man who really loves does not spare the one he loves, you claim. And that just shows how little you feel when you refuse to fight with —your woman. Keeping for the night your envy and your hate.

But I want to interpret your midnight dreams, and unmask that phenomenon: your night. And make you admit that I dwell in it as your most fearsome adversity. So that you can finally realize what your greatest ressentiment is. And so that with you I can fight to make the earth my own, and stop allowing myself to be a slave to your nature. And so that you finally stop wanting to be the only god.

For isn't that the way the State begins —with war between men alone? The State—that cold monster that claims to be the people and, over the heads of the herds, hangs a belief in love and the sword of desire.* The State that speaks of good and evil in a single language and, in that one language, decrees only lies. For there is no common language that speaks the truth. And the State has stolen his language from each individual and then mixed them all up in one death wish.

Such is the attraction and seduction of that new idol—it rids each one of his own will and promises a happy life to anyone weary of fighting his god.

It promises to take charge of everything as long as you promise in return to give up the brilliance of your virtue and the look in your proud eyes.

And it wants you heroes on its side to lure the masses and drag

---

*"State is the name of the coldest of all cold monsters. Coldly it tells lies too; and this lie crawls out of its mouth: 'I, the state, am the people.' That is a lie! It was creators who created peoples and hung a faith and a love over them: thus they served life" (*The Portable Nietzsche*, p. 160).—Tr.

25

good men and bad to their doom. And when they all slowly kill and are killed, that is the State's invention—a way of dying that is mistaken for life itself.

But still there remains many a place on the earth for solitary men and solitary pairs. There sea winds still blow and the irreplaceable and unique melody of the simply necessary can still be sung.*

Thus you speak, calling for men to lay down all their possessions. To go beyond all burdens and prisons of a power that rests its throne upon human sacrifice.

And (you) entice men to gaze up at the rainbow and the bridge, laughing at anyone that gives up the lofty air to serve the new idol. And (you) preach the meaning of the earth.

☆

But your greatest sorrow and your greatest disgust are reserved for me. And in order to return to the depths of the earth, you still need to get back through the skin sickness that keeps you apart. That you covered her with to prevent you from wanting to move back inside her. That keeps you far away in ressentiment.

This sickness of man. But that he gives as security for what he is leaving behind and claiming to rise above. Veiling his nostalgia in contempt. And vomiting up that first nurse whose milk and blood he has drunk.

But of your contempt (I) shall make a thread to find my way back. In what you vomit up, (I) shall seek out what you're giving back to me. By interpeting your contempt, I shall find my skin again. Washing off the disguises of wretchedness.

This is fortune! That in your excrement I must read the sign of my greatness. In your distance, the extent of my realm. And in your will to destroy, the will to reduce to nothingness anything that might tie you to me by a necessity of first and last hour. To destroy actively what you had to give up in order to be a man. To annihilate the body that gave you life, and that still keeps you living.

And your whole will, your eternal recurrence, are these anything more than the dream of one who neither wants to have been born, nor to continue being born, at every instant, of a female other? Does

---

*"The earth is free even now for great souls. There are still many empty seats for the lonesome and the twosome, fanned by the fragrance of silent seas" (*The Portable Nietzsche*, p. 163).—Tr.

your joy in becoming not result from annihilating her from whom you are tearing yourself away?

Eternal is the joy that carries within it the joy of annihilation, the affirmation of destruction. In which the negative changes its sign and becomes its opposite for a new mode of being. In which man, as he reproduces himself, himself produces his becoming. Reversing the process of his generation. Wanting to create the universal of all becoming? Beyond physics. A superb distance from the birth that remains natural.

Eternity, that is the music of one who senses and fears decline. And, for passing beyond life and death, see how busily he is at work at this moment. To leave his body behind and fly away unburdened, isn't this always and forever the point of his creation?

So, whether it be your eternity or another, what does it matter! Isn't it still a ghost's desire rather than a living being's? And to transmute beyond the body? Without stopping in this life.

And it's true, the "you" (tu) is older than the "I." But this "you" is not your neighbor.* What is surrounding you at present is only showy rubbish. Or the trash and human waste of a much older man.

That's what your love of your neighbor is like. And your pity for those paltry remains of something very far away that you chase after.

You're looking too close to yourself. You're looking too close to find the love that gave you birth. Too close to attract and savor some semblance of being. Whereas from the future comes back a ghost in search of flesh and bones.

What is this fear that seizes you at its approach? And what makes you hurry over to your neighbor's house? Are you going there to find or to lose yourself? And what distant places pay the expense of your anguish of solitude? Who dies every time you (vous) stand together in that way?

---

*"The *you* is older than the *I*; the *you* has been pronounced holy, but not yet the *I*; so man crowds toward his neighbor" (*The Portable Nietzsche*, p. 172).—Tr.

And aren't these comedies and puppet shows you (vous) state when, behind closed doors, you rejoice in the oblivion of being alone?

And if there still exists one friend who finds no escape route in such shows and whose heart overflows to see the world end, he still stands firm, like a shell of goodness that wants to make you (vous) a present of his world. And espouses only one who espouses the fullness of his world by drinking it in. Willing to be your origin and your end. And entrusting you, for love's own sake, with the future of his destiny.

## AN AIRY GRAVE

And walking long within me through every dimension but always to the rhythm of your own footsteps, you have dragged me into such suffering that, to survive, (I) have become still and indifferent. Impassive ground. You can take possession of me as the whim takes you, you're only taking over an earth with no other nature than your own. You're just drawing on the apparently neutral reserves you still use to protect yourself a little from destruction.

But this inert matter you exploit for your disguises, these props you use for your various character parts, are they not in fact a sign of your annihilation? And when you have again and again surrounded yourself with lifeless layers of air, won't you be separated from the movement of all life? As you move forward in the security of those unseen burials, of those unfelt embalmer's bands, you are carrying death to everything you approach. This is the worst peril today: the death that is taken for life. This death that you forced upon me so that you could control it and resist it and which now pushes us aside into a mere appearance of living beings.

And I have suffered the violence of your passions so many times that often peaceful serenity tries me. I am lifeless but deprived of yet living my death. Indefinitely in death. A mourning veil into which you endlessly transfigure me so as to make yourself immortal. Dwelling in death without every dying, I keep for you the dream—of being able to overcome your body. And this ideal—not to feel life passing by. Neither to suffer from nor even to imagine the matter from which life is made, and unmade. And to descend into the depths of your existence to ask you the question of your sustenance.

"Wherein am I a living man?", isn't that the question that you always evade, preferring to inquire: "How can I survive?" You always stand outside your present hour.

But he who has gone through pain, is free of heaviness. Miraculous is the motion of him who, beyond nostalgia, goes on walking. And what once was a burden has become a bad dream dissolving in a mist. The events and earthly powers that once haunted him touch him only as light air that may be captured once and for all in painted figures, generating fascinating ghosts.

The man who discovers what such ills are made of, and resolves their enigma himself rather than laying their burden on the other, is suddenly moving in a world with no boundaries but those of his living body.

At that point is the beginning of the man whose highest achievement is to be what he is. With no evasion. And, as long as the other of himself appears to him only as a shadow to overcome, as a river to get over, he will still miss his footing, tightrope walker that he is.

And how, from then on, he longs for the earth who will let him regain his balance! How he loves and dares her who gives him back his weight. How afraid he is to find in her the holes he dug as he came into the world. How he is haunted by the desire to find his place back in the tomb.

And how he leaves you (vous), his other, in charge in order to get as far away as he can. So, as he comes back toward you, he is chained into an oscillating pattern of ever faster and broader comings and goings.

And his movements are both paralyzed and crazy as he runs. And he trembles when you (vous) say to him: you have still not begun to live. Now begin again, starting with the earth, and remember to be a man. And don't hurry to escape yourself by wiping the other out of your consciousness. Making that act of negation into a cradle of night in which you can dwell within you-the-other-self (en toi-l'autre). For the shadow or the ghost of what one kills always comes back, like a double hunting you down.

And because you don't distinguish yourself from the other, you are now sinking down as in a current, so you can barely come up for air. And as soon as that brief moment of alertness is over, you (tu) dive back into her who bears you, and never do you break completely free of her. For that is not your fortune!

And that mother is not at all opposed to your managing, once you have parted from her, to realize in yourself the form she sketched out for you, or to your perfecting the features she gave you at birth, as long you do not use death masks to achieve all this.

A death mask is the forgetting of one's birth, the passion for routine, the repeating of an order that stops development dead, and the law of final ends.

☆

And the fact that your unique necessity is death is what keeps us apart. Whereas you finish all (female) things off by wrapping them in an airy shroud, I leave them open so that they can go on breathing and respond to the sap that feeds them. So they can flower over and over again. Attentive to the becoming whereby sometimes they (elles) open and sometimes close, wake up or fall asleep according to time and season, stretching up to the light or resting in the shade as the sun moves across the sky.

Never marshaled into flower beds, never lined up in a single border, they (elles) appear every moment for the first time. Which is not to say that at every moment they are overjoyed about a becoming that, for them, takes place in air whose transparency surrounds their growth without ever freezing it.

In this way I never bathe in the same air, except when you capture me in your unique mirror. But the beauty you seduce thus is only a showy facade under which I still dwell.

Unless you have dragged me into your death forever and I have given up living in order to obey your necessity. That way I have become your idea, and have no roots other than those of your thought.

30

Eternally the slave of the becoming of your thought. Forever veiled in your airy productions.

But I want to disentangle myself from your appearances, unravel again and again the mirages conjured up by your seductiveness, and find where I begin once more.

See how far I am going away. Since going beyond your will draws me farther than the farthest you can go. Outside of your circle. Slipping out of your sight so that I can return to my birth.

And how incredibly bare I am becoming, and undetectable to the eye that has forgotten the body where it takes place. And what a hole in your memory is made when I come back to myself. How deep into forgetting you must dig to find the memory of a place where I had not yet entered your horizon.

You rub your eyes, anxious to know if I am a ghost or a living woman. If I have ever existed, if your memory is other than a dream.

Leave your gaze open, nothing is changed in it. Have I ever been anything but your dream of midday or midnight?

But if I go away, will you finally awake? Or will you find some other woman to hang your light to? Not even noticing the difference.

And how can I remind you of the place where what you never notice wells up inexhaustibly? Of that beyond that leaves me in shadow. And shuts me up in the blind mirror of what I give you.

Is this not the worst reversal of all, to make me mimic your mirages and cease to be that hearth which gives you birth? And doesn't your gaze reduce me to your images or illusions?

Why are we not, the one for the other, a resource of life and air? Celebrations and springing out of or into the same. And beyond what I am and you are, a glow of heat and light that never exhausts the end of its hours.

## ICE WEDDING

All right, so you want her to signify: you are the being of becoming. But do you make that same statement in return, for her? Do you confide in her: you are the becoming of being?

31

If talking that way still has a meaning.

Because, in her, becoming and being never join up in the shape of a ring. But the movement whereby becoming remains becoming without ever forming a circle under-lies the possibility of any alliance.

And, in the eternal recurrence, she attends your wedding celebration, she takes part in it, but you yourself are bride and groom. She keeps hold of the thread, anchors the harmony, sings the tune. An accompaniment that is necessary to you while remaining fundamentally reactive as long as you do not also allow her her self.

Thus, throughout all the wedding ceremonies, you hoard an essential ressentiment. Of course you pass it off on an other, pass it into or through an other, whether that other be your ass or your camel, or . . . , all that is clear. But in the end, what does it matter! Of them you have need and desire. With them too your sublimest feasts are played out. And still you have not given up the joy of heavy loads. That other knows it, she who always has a good strong back and stays faithful to you through all the pirouettings of your soul.

And if, at the end of your hour, she has again to carry the load of what you have created—a mere simulacrum of becoming—what do you care if her back is broken by the weight, as long as she still has the strength to give that present back, in the shape of a sounding echo that the voice of her flesh fills out.

But, when she gives you back the fabric of your destiny, she risks cutting off its thread. Once you are lighter than air, having jettisoned that link to matter and sustenance, where will you fly now? What illusion will draw you higher than your highest day?

If from her you want confirmation for your being, why don't you let her explore its labyrinths? Why don't you give her leave to speak? From the place where she sings the end of your becoming, let her be able to tell you: no. Still you wish to return into nothingness, alone it lures you on like your highest dream. Now begin again, come back to your becoming, and cease to take mine away from me. Let us be merry/marry together at last!

And of course it's true that she can send you back the melancholy effects of your self-marriage. But isn't this a strange love you are preaching: love for a looking glass eternally set opposite you. That is your most sublime fortune.

And if you found your reflection with her in a river that you would set flowing together, isn't that a feast you're forgetting, o modern man, devoted to appearances.

That she can finally become your mirror is today your chief article of faith. These weddings of yours are always of light, drought, and hardness. And (you) want to shine rather than burn, freeze rather than flow, hold back over and again instead of flowing endlessly outward. And eternity, for you, is only your indefinitely repeated mirage. Your innocence wills it thus!

But your innocence also wills that you should never speak to her, to the one whom you give everything and whom you entrust for present and future with the redoubling of your affirmation. And all she may say to you is: yes.

From this "yes" of her flesh that is always given and proffered to suit your eternity, you draw your infinite reserves of veils and sails, of wings and flight... Of sublimation and dissimulation. For this flesh that is never spoken—either by you or by her—remains a ready source of credulity for your fantasies.

It is because she never says anything but "yes" to your all that you are able to go off so far, so high, soaring up in your dream life. Spreading her out, folding her up, securing her, letting her flap freely, according to your fortune, or to the weather you're having, the wind that's blowing for you, the rain or storm of the moment. Once she is deflowered, you can draw infinitely upon her for your weaving, your painting, your writing, your music too... For the beauty you create.

Since, in your eyes, her beauty can take place only once, she will henceforth only attract you by pretending and disguising the ways in which she sustains you.

But is that not your twilight—this nature that already mimics, for you, the dissimulation that attracts you? How will you imitate her if she is covered up by your workings and reduced to a superficial existence—your essential desire. If, having become skeptical, she merges into disguises that suit your taste and distaste for her—the deep one. If, for the future of your decline, she now wants merely to put in an appearance, create an illusion, a trick, putting a price on

33

your power that discounts on delusions. If you finally unload onto her the weight of your subject, but in order to make her trumpet the aim of your ultimate difference: the achievement of becoming, that is to say all or nothing. A snake that gnaws on its own tail and ecstatically welcomes this return upon the self.

☆

To overcome the impossible of your desire—that is surely your last hour's desire. Giving birth to such and such a production, or such and such a child is a summary of your history. But to give birth to your desire itself, that is your final thought. To be incapable of doing it, that is your highest ressentiment. For you either make works that fit your desire, or you make desire itself into your work. But how will you find the material to produce such a child?

And, going back to the source of all your children, you want to bring yourself back into the world. As a father? or a child? And isn't being two at a time the point where you come unstuck? Because, to be a father, you have to produce, procreate, your seed has to escape and fall from you. You have to engender suns, dawns, and twilights other than your own.

But in fact isn't it your will, in the here and now, to pull everything back inside you and to be and to have only one sun? And to fasten up time, for you alone? And suspend the ascending and descending movement of genealogy? And to join up in one perfect place, one perfect circle, the origin and end of all things?

But things have a beginning and end. And where your child begins, there your body is reproduced and finished. And those two bodies cannot only make one.

And even though your children have a place only in your words, yet they still escape you, and those little beings wander far away from you.

And if, wishing to keep everything inside you, you sow seed in your own mouth, doesn't that masterly trick reduce you to silence? To thwarting your own ecstasies—isn't that your highest will?

And you ask a woman to help you in this operation. To redouble your affirmation. To give yourself back as a unit—subjects and objects of all your ecstasy. To fold all your becoming back into your being. To give you back, in the here and now, everything you have believed, loved, produced, planned, been. . .

Everything that you have believed, loved, produced, planned, been . . . and the place whence and where that had taken place. All those sunbeams and everything that attracted them, that was bathed in them, that was lit up, enlightened, quickened by them. . . Let everything return to hearth and home and may you finally stand firm within yourself, losing nothing of your warmth or your light—neither tropism nor sowing. To be at last the crucible of all suns and all sources.

May she ensure that power for you with a "yes" in which she appears and disappears as pure obedience to your will.

☆

And rewinding the thread of time amounts to recapitulating all desires and their subjects, acts, and objects, here and now. Two ecstasies—at least—are folded up in a pressing summons of the being of your becoming: a summons that brings you out of yourself and that in which you are made flesh.

Two returns, therefore. To have no further wish to move out of the self, to have no attraction except for oneself in different modes of desirability. To sense only oneself in the other, only desire of the self in the desire of the other. And, in the end, to cease desiring, but be the achieved object of one's own desire as reflected by a female other. Cease all attraction, all movement toward, but have a well-positioned double accomplice who sends you back all causes and effects of what you are desiring or might desire here and now.

By holding yourself again here and now, you hold yourself back from producing. You reproduce your self twice over: as subject and effect of your will, as will to power and eternal recurrence.

## THE REVERSE SIDE OF YOUR LIMIT

That is the being of your becoming, valuable only through the permanence of her "yes": spoken to each one of your links, as to the

35

whole chain, to each moment of the becoming as it is to the being, to your chances as to your sole necessity.

But since, twisting back upon yourself this way, you have neither tail nor mouth, it is left to her to reflect your destiny as superman.

Thus, when finally you allow her to speak, it is only to bring about —your perspective, your art, your time, your will. The last pattern of your being that she must still reproduce or mimic. And this takes her away from her surfaces, her depths. Her face, her lips, her world of harmony, her tuneful flow mastered by your creation. All these are veiled or bent to suit your viewpoint. She is cut off from herself in this way in order to join in your game. Becoming speech in your mouth, a stranger in her own body. As motionless as you can wish, she speaks the "yes" dictated to her by your latest movement, your latest will, your final plastic necessity. Her song accompanies and celebrates the latest work your music has paused at.

Henceforth you would be separated from her only by a single membrane. And even so. . . Through that membrane, might you not, with some wonder and horror, discover the back that corresponds to your front? Your silence is brushing the bottom of something it had thought never to touch again. You are now immersed and reenveloped in something that erases all boundaries. Carried away by the waves. Drowning in the flood. Tragic castaway in unrestrained turmoil.

☆

Such is the failure of the man who does not make his own boundary out of the skin of the other. He is turned back to the other side of his limit. A catastrophe that would have no place to be if he obeyed the music of that female other. If he let her carry him along without forcing her to follow his rhythm alone.

For anyone who does nothing but obey ceases to be heard. And if the one and the other are not joined in the difference of their movements, they risk the abyss one within the other, no longer sensing anything either of the same or of the other.

The one in the other, they fall back. And at the end, no sails, no skiff, no bridge remain in that breaking up and thawing of ice. And anyone who always relied on solid ground and stout moorings and lifejackets and who hung on to good and evil, to truth, illusion, pretense . . . and also to the meaning of the earth, is now drowning in a pleasure (jouissance) that he has not willed. He who balanced on the highest peaks, on a rope, on thin air, and still managed to keep his footing, is now sinking.

For there is no peril greater than the sea. Everything is constantly moving and remains eternally in flux. Hence with a thawing wind, bad fortune arrives. As well as salvation.

And in order for you to be pleasured, without always seeking pleasure (jouissance) anywhere else but in me, let the ice break up now. Let us be done with believing we need flints which only open up the solid shells of your ideas, or spurs to get your impassive things moving.

In me everything is already flowing, and you flow along too if you only stop minding such unaccustomed motion, and its song. Learn to swim, as once you danced on dry land, for the thaw is much nearer at hand than you think. And what ice could resist your sun? And, before it disappears, perhaps chance will have the ice enflame you, dissolving your hardness, melting your gold.

So remember the liquid ground. And taste the saliva in your mouth also—notice her familiar presence during your silence, how she is forgotten when you speak. Or again: how you stop speaking when you drink. And how necessary all of that is for you!

These fluids softly mark the time. And there is no need to knock, just listen to hear the music. With very small ears.

And when you want your spring to be lost in the sea, what do you say? You have already dwelt in the sea. Isn't streaming into the sea a return to the same? Isn't it going back to the spring from whence you have sprung? Why be so horrified at the prospect? Why wouldn't you go back to drink from your first nurse? Why would you not give her like and other drink in return? And the unceasing movement of two springs feeding each other could be the pledge of eternal happiness, could it not? When the ascending and the descending meet in the rapture of their marriage? Beyond erection and decline. Beyond high and low, and their hollows and abysses.

And if never, as on the eve of your first morning, you return to that nurse, where is your source? Where have you drawn what flows out of you? Only from your own yesterday and today?

And isn't it by forgetting the first waters that you achieve immersion in your abysses and the giddy flight of one who wings far away, perched at such heights that no sap rises there and no thread secures his way.

Of course, that is your fortune—to play with fire. And become harder than metal tempered in the furnace. But anything too rigid often breaks. And when the time of the thaw comes, it rusts away in the waters.

Could it be that the unexplored reaches of the farthest ocean are now your most dangerous beyond? Though they lie just outside your present project. No doubt they promise new discoveries. But will you not need to move beyond yourself, lowering your sail even, if you are to approach an other sight? For the man who searches too hard within the compass of his sails finds only what he has already found, and lost.

## THE SONG OF THE CICADA

Over there, appearing and disappearing behind the clouds, your mountain peaks have the transparency of a dream. And your glaciers seem like pictures gilded by the setting sun, half covered in mist. Soon will come evening. Soon the time to stretch out on the ground and accomplish other dreams. Come back down from your mountain. It will be cold there tonight. And even if you are not afraid to be alone in the dark and chill of your cave, at least remember that you need some other light and heat than those of your sun. And if you wish to muse over your great thoughts tomorrow, come back here and sleep a little.

Do not forget the thoughts of mid-night. If tomorrow you wish to return your ultimate depth to the day and hear the voice of your abyss rise up to you, come back and sink into my silence. There you will be able to vomit up the excess of today's discourse and innocence will be reborn. You will be able to chatter or speak your latest thought, break or flow like a dead man, and tomorrow will see you with a soul that has slipped out of today's restraints. Your being's fences mended, you will be able to go off again when you will, eternally faithful to yourself.

And (I) shall in no way reproach you for your lack of fidelity. In no way try to hold you back by the thread of compassion. Nor shall (I) ask you for any mercy on this new morning.

For I have learned at least this much from your wisdom: when the other does not hear you, it is better to be silent. By doing violence to the ear, one loses the music.

But who stole that wisdom from the other? And might it not be she whom you come back to seek at night? The persistence of a silence that would not be obedience. The sound of lips pressed together being sweeter harmony for you than all the fine speeches that merely sicken the appetite. And when she sings endlessly, filling the air with plenteous profusion without ever speaking or breaking, could this be your nostalgia?

But it is the nostalgia for woman that you preach and that haunts you beyond your resolves.

☆

So go to the women, and forget your leading strings. For you will hear nothing of women as long you are bending them thus to your will.

But you will never have pleasure (jouir) in woman, if you insist on being woman. If you insist on making her a stage in your process. There is nothing like unto women. They go beyond all simulation. And when they are copied, the abyss remains. Far short of your measurements, the abandoned ones, the women, have their place.

And even when you come to them to find something, you still stop on the way, and thereby leave your best part behind. For example you believe that those guardian women are always pregnant. And sit down to await what of you is about to be born. Whereas in fact the women are singing emptiness, like cicadas that rub their wings together in the fine weather.

That music of a present lacking in nothing—which is not to say that it possesses everything—remains foreign to you. You love woman

39

from afar, but fear her close at hand. For her goods exceed your riches. And even if, within her, you had poured your all, still (she) would smile in sadness. And pity you for having received so much of your need.

And, in the laughing sky of her eyes, it is not a desire for yet more riches that lights the gleam of nostalgia. Abundance looking over the seas and seeking and waiting still. For what matter your riches!

And she is not athirst to be full with child nor needful of being delivered! But that you should sometimes remember her and embrace her without wanting to fill her to the brim, overwhelm her with your gifts. Let her return to the rhythm of her blood. To that happiness in living that remains a mystery to you. And that you do not want to receive from her.

She it is who attracts as she moves away, stops you as she seeks you out, you who love to suffer and for whom the cold is brazier, hatred is charm, flight is bond, sarcasm—emotion. That is your fortune! The death that must dress life up to make it desirable.

If it were not for the lure of death, would you rise up? Without the fear and fascination of death, would you speak your solemn word aloud so that others may receive it even if you are broken by it? Without the peril of death, would you want children? Yet isn't it equally because you fear death that you want no children?

And (you) go and come, want the there here and here there, come near as you veer away, find the closest in the furthest, sidle up from a distance, give and withhold, unable to stop the play of your contradictions. It is your fortune that life and death are forever entwined, that the one and the other together move you. And that, no sooner do you run after the one, than the other seizes your will. Eternally an infernal dance is danced within you. But it is your own! And ever the same and identical it begins once again.

For you must always be climbing up and then back down, down and then back up, filling up, emptying out, letting your waters flow out so that you may drink. And the one and the other cannot take place exactly at the same moment. The one and the other always end up as the one to the other, turning the wheel without turning up at the same time. Except to abolish your will.

Your duplicity can never be surpassed, nor your nostalgia for the being of becoming and of eternity. And yet (you) will die before that recurrence. For your fortune cannot do without a beginning and an end. Or without that ascending and descending chronology.

And giving up good and evil will not change anything. Beyond good and evil, you are still motivated by the same movement. And that alternation sets the beat for your time more implacably when you have no wish but your will, no salvation but your own fortune.

## DANCE OF THE ABYSS

And life is never identical to itself, but death is. At least one may imagine it so: with nothing happening anymore. And by preaching the eternal recurrence, you are broken as a living man. Your fate is to go to your ruin as you proffer your solemn word. Heralding something that can only take place after you, and without you: the being of your becoming. In this pressing appeal, you proclaim your decline. You bring your cycle to a close.

For life never stays still. And if life doesn't flourish, it fades. Either you discover more and more new sources of life, or you walk toward the grave. Becoming always remains unstable. And take care, o man, if you don't strive to become more living, you are already more dead. It takes only a moment for the scales to shift. For you to find yourself moving down the slope. All it needs is for you to forget that you cannot stop or overcome the movement of life.

But hasn't the will to do so always dictated your speeches? Don't you choose to die in each of your words so that you may survive in them? That is your fortune! And the more death you create, the higher you believe yourself to be.

But you who think endlessly about the passage of time, what in your past are you avenging? Death is still to come. In front of you, it is coming. On one single occasion the unique one will accost you. And you will no longer be there to feel any ressentiment. You won't even need to digest death. Let others mourn for you.

So what worries you in eternity? Are you still wishing yourself some kind of God? Yes? No? To be God? So that none may have power of creation over you? Wanting yourself as your own all? The All? Living? Or dead? Or both? And what if you had to make a choice?

You have made a choice: your only wife is eternity. And as for living, what does it matter! If that means sharing. Mourning at times for some desire?

But don't living and dying involve permanent mourning? At each step, don't you have to give up the previous step taken? And don't you endlessly come back to haunt that step so as to prevent its completion? So as to take back the desire that had taken place there. And are you not convinced you have lived everything when you have not even begun to live?

At the end of your hour, (you) will still not have completed a single step because you keep going back over the same (one). What are you unable to abandon? What place are you unwilling to leave? What weight always holds you back at the same point? The will to live or to die?

In mourning for life? Or for death? Are you coming back to drink at the spring or to repeat endlessly the step that leads you away from it? Aren't you mixing the two up in the same? And what if you had to make a choice?

That is your impossible dilemma. Because to receive, without swallowing up what has been given to you in your own process, without taking revenge on what you have assimilated by wishing yourself to be the all—that is the cycle of your recurrence. And (you) prefer not to have begun to live rather than to have received birth. That is the will of your living on.

And that the other has given you what escapes your creation is the source of your highest ressentiment. How to bring the gift of life, that is the question you ponder upon your mountain top. How to be unique and gather all sources into the self. And you rise ever higher, believing that fertility can only come down from the sky! That is your incredible naïveté, o man of the mountain peaks, neglectful of other landscapes.

☆

So climb. Again. The spring is far behind you. Come back to drink at night.

And swiftly you pour out your riches and swiftly you go off again, full of nostalgia. Have you not discovered what you were looking for? What did you want? To give life or to take it? Give life back, or take it back? And what if you had to make a choice? Impossible? Whereas in fact are you not giving what you give and taking what you take? You don't want to? You want it all at the same moment? And to eliminate differences. And to wipe out contraries, overcome opposites? To give life—to give death, to receive life—to receive death, these amount to the same for you? But where does your greatest strength come from, and where does it go? And your highest will?

And simply because you must always abandon something, unload your surpluses, drop your seed or your fruit, means no doubt that you never give. Merging with the object of your gift. Identified and lost in your bounty. And wanting it to be received for nothing, except thanks.

You give in order to. In order to survive? Survive yourself? And become at last the all—immutable and identical to yourself?

But you never reach the point of giving yourself. New beginnings and new failures always accompany that operation. Always you both want and do not want to keep yourself. You want and do not want to lose yourself. To remain master of your projects. Subject of your creations, so as to achieve greater sovereignty over them perhaps? And as your only wife, you want eternity. For in her, finally (you) can give yourself up wholly. Though dead.

Because you cannot overcome the relation of the whole to the part while being a living man, wanting to live. Your body can never overcome that part of you that is called man and that drives your will. The one and the other are often at war. One must be annihilated or broken. And the two cannot unite into one whole entity.

Is that the fortune of women? And the reason why you want them under the guise of eternity? Why you blame them for still being alive and yet whole at every moment of their becoming. As the movements that most matter to them never separate from the place where they (elles) take place. Remaining within the whole they inhabit. Going and coming in the body that they live. And their love never has to drag them forcibly out of themselves.

Unless they wish to make a man. Give up their fortune! And that happens when they seek to be like you or to please you. When they dress up at your request. Putting on veils and becoming mere decoration just to attract you.

But that kind of attractiveness takes them far from themselves. They forget the luck they have—to be born women.

☆

And your nostalgia means that, outside of women, you never complete your first step. Before establishing its completion, you stop. Before any boundaries can be marked, before any first distance away from women can be established to distinguish your shapes, you cease walking.

Between the time your first step sets off and arrives, you stop to dance. Between the one and the other, on a tightrope that holds you up, you jump. Higher and higher, marking time to the beat on the spot. Farther and farther away, sure of returning to the same point.

But it is within one step that the soaring of your rhythm is lost. And if you find the strength to dash forward along the path of your recurrence, you always risk the abyss.

Because remaining halfway between the beginning and the end implies the will to overcome the affirmation and negation of distance, doubling them by means of your repeated flight. But, in this setting, neither the one nor the other are encountered or inhabited. And, by refusing to separate the two, you lose both.

So it happens that you believe that between the one and the other is the void. The effect of difference is so powerful that its misperception reams out bottomless chasms.

Two steps, then, at least. And no one step. Nothing came of the difference between the one and the other. You remain within the same. From the dimensions, horizontal and vertical, that you trace as you break away and move in close, you complete your circle.

At the center you dance, upon a nothing in common. That is your mistress. You leap up and down with the elasticity of a band that is ready to snap back as strongly as it is being stretched away from its point of inertia.

You bustle around so much just to keep on the move! You keep so busy to avoid paralysis! You need to keep scurrying about right and left, up and down to escape the feeling of weight in your body!

And to the lure of the void under your steps you respond by trying to make yourself lighter than air. So that you don't plummet down like a stone.

And you hold on so tightly to your circle as if it stopped you falling! Turning endlessly above the abyss, and finding in that movement a fragile equilibrium.

And if the other breaks the thread, what a fearful end! For today no God holds you up from heaven. As for being, does it amount to anything more than some puffs of air or melted wax if the other flees the house?

☆

And from me you never move away. Always you seek to return into that land. Always you want to be born. But to give life also. Do you imagine that you are giving life by running in and out like that all the time? Does receiving or taking life mean giving it? To whom? And do I owe you thanks for having brought you back into the world so many times?

Did she, your first woman, have need to pour out into you the overflow of her riches? Did she win more life by nourishing you with her blood? Or is she thereby marked with the death that she has thus attributed to herself? She whom death does not belong to. Who is bent down under your death. Feeling its approach only when that body that she is bearing falls from her.

And is it not good fortune to rest and recover, when that hour has been accomplished? And ill fortune that living inwardness that keeps tearing away from her so as to weave the web of its appearances?

And doesn't she prefer death to life when endlessly she runs after that burden, anxious to pick it up and carry it once more? As if her body lacked the power of attraction. As if you had to give her her gravity? Or leave her your weight? When you fly away, doesn't something still have to tie you to the earth?

45

## HER ULTIMATE DEPTH NEVER RETURNS TO
## THE LIGHT OF DAY

And the sea can shed shimmering scales indefinitely. Her depths peel off into innumerable thin, shining layers. And each one is the equal of the other as it catches a reflection and lets it go. As it preserves and blurs. As it captures the glinting play of light. As it sustains mirages. Multiple and still far too numerous for the pleasure of the eye, which is lost in that host of sparkling surfaces. And with no end in sight.

And these surfaces are all equally deep and superficial. Unless one of them is made into a bridge that holds a person up, prevents him from sinking, that crosses over but never penetrates.

And they all reflect the same (le même), if they are found at the same time and place. Which is both necessary and impossible. They move together, but they cover each other over and are never separated from one another. It is artifice to spell the depths out one by one. And the sharpest knife has no effect. As soon as the knife slices in, they (elles) close up unwearyingly, and the blade leaves not even a trace.

What a limitless world of appearances lies concealed beneath the great seas! If a man wants to delude himself, the sea will always lend him the sails to fit his fortune. And the (female) one and the other change places constantly without the one ever being really superior to the other. As they imperceptibly tint the whole with a skin of light that has the color of the moment.

And because her depths are high, and deeper than the day has imagined, anyone who finds in her the efflorescent source of his dreams rises very high, drawn higher than his highest day.

And when, in her abundance, she is not giving waters—those supple living envelopes for specular alchemy—she gives forth airs. And, according to the weather, she can become ice or restless waves. She is hard or melting at the whim of sun or wind.

And from her is born the very crystal that dream fixed in its transparent brilliance. Enigmatic fish, sleeping in her abysses and that even the wiliest fisherman will have trouble catching. Life beneath the sea is not fed upon honey even. Its own elements suffices it.

But the loftiest gaze does not penetrate thus far into her depths and is still unable to unfold all the membranes she offers to bathe his contemplations.

And whoever looks upon her from the overhanging bank finds there a call to somewhere farther than his farthest far. Toward an other ever more other. Beyond any anchorage yet imaginable. Any landing at the appearance of one of her strata.

As she unfurls, casting off all moorings. Her waves rolling again and yet again over one another. Stirring with strength as far as she extends.

And (she is) much deeper than the day ever conceived her to be. For days sets before touching the sea bottom. Before it can set anchor even at the last hour. The sea blushes at this setting sun that is forever tangent to sea swell but she still remains dark.

Anything that has not yet seen daylight hurtles into the abyss. Anything that remains unillumined is taken by the eye to be a chasm drawing a man to his destruction. And since he does not want to fall, he comes back at break of dawn to get a good look at things and thereby ensure himself a firm footing as he goes off again on his high-seas explorations. Expecting, further and later on, to come upon the shore of the furthest land.

But (he) keeps going on and keeps coming back, and never gets there. The sea is too deep. Hiding away from the final landfall. And anyone who wants her to send him back her deepest depths is lost. For one by one each of her surfaces takes its turn to shimmer. And the mirage falls into the gleaming abyss, endlessly.

The sea shines with a myriad eyes. And none is given any privilege. Even here and now she undoes all perspective. Countless and shifting and merging her depths. And her allure is an icy shroud for the point of view.

No rapture, no peril, is greater than that of the sea. And the man has still to come who will live that love out beyond the reach of any port. Letting go of his rock, his ship, his island, and even of that last drop of oil on the water, and all so that he can feel the intoxication of such vastness.

☆

Rather do the boldest navigators prefer to dry the sea, and spread their sails at her expense. They draw, endlessly, upon her reserves to push their skiff along.

And as they advance deeper out into the waves, the mariners discover the tumult of higher dreams. The thirst of loftier thoughts. The call to still-unheard-of truths. A siren song drawing them away from any shore. Short of any landfall.

Even the most intrepid tie themselves to the mast, for fear of succumbing to the spell of the undauntable one. And they want to drive their prows over her. But her depths are never ploughed by their blades. Which barely cleave the crest of her waves.

And their passage leaves no permanent trace. Once they are gone, she returns to her rhythm and her measure. Even as their ships cross over her, yet she remains. the same. Incorruptible. And she laughs as they move onward, seeking the secret of their truth. When they get close to it, they don't notice it. They just keep moving on, in search of something that offers a solid resistance and opposition to their wandering. That offers a rampart to beat back their thought.

Fluid and flaming as she is, are they not impatient to dry her up? To contain her in some enclosure where she finds her end. And thus be captive, stifled within the narrow limits of their perspectives.

Delirium of language, the boldest navigators. With their hulls and sails, don't they want to take possession of all depths?

But (she) instantly perishes when taken away from her shifting bed. If transparency is frozen, is she not already deprived of the permanence of her becoming? Torn away from the place which gives place to her. No sooner is she brought to the light of day than she fades into mere appearance. And the most skillful fisherman can see only the scales of death in her.

Already those sea lovers have pulled out thousands of such fish. And it is their sadness and their triumph that they can still pull death out of her over and over again. Will they ever get to the bottom? And determined to force that enigma, they continue to return to the sea, hoping to take her last fish.

But it may be that wholly (tout entière) she is not yet theirs. That her mystery remains whole. Has yet to appear to them. Because her ultimate depth does not return to the light of day. And the voice of her abysses is not to be folded and gathered up into a single thought. Rather it (elle) will bring down every sail already chartered, if it makes itself heard.

For there is no higher call than the sea's. The man who can no longer hear it, has already lost his hearing to her spell. And hears only the sea, and hears no longer. But moves blindly in search of its source.

Those wanderers in deep waters sometimes get closer to their destinations than voyagers who leave port better prepared. Prows slicing through the water, masts crowding the sky, sails cunningly set, a firm hand on the helm, (they) go straight to the shore. Such proud vessels keep their heading. And how they resist the sea! And always find the way home. And never go to sea again. Those lofty navigators, alpinists of the high seas.

And whatever the weather, they keep their heads cool, and their feet dry, mastering the storm by the skillful set of their sails. And if one sail tears, quickly they hoist another. And have enough rigged not to drift. And a thick enough hull not to go under.

Of all the winds on the high seas they have learned to make their playthings. To spread their store of canvas according to the direction of the gusts, the gale raging, the squalls lowering. For these sea lovers always use sail. And sometimes the worst happens: they have to lower all sails to prevent them from tearing. And they miss the resource of spread canvas surfaces.

An hour of anxious suspense. The proudest navigators wait and pray. How needy and suppliant they are in this moment. How afraid they are the sea will swallow them up. How unprepared they find themselves to face this unchaining of natural forces. And what good is all their seamanship if the sea refuses to submit to it? What good is their language if there is nothing and no one to appeal to? And who will rescue them from the whirlwind sown by their own presumptuousness?

Might they not then be found bent toward the ground, faced with their nothingness, and warding off the abysses? And let no one preach immortality to them at that moment. Let no one tell them that it is divine to throw oneself into the sea—to forget. And who at that moment still thinks of flying upward, in free rapture? Who is still dancing on that heaving deck? Who is still resting within some mirror? And will their final prayer be addressed to the sun? Will their final chance of life rely on the gaze?

And don't they try to shake off their paralysis? Rigid with fear, don't they yet endeavor to go through the motions that might still save them? To melt the numbness gripping their bodies, even as the sea hypnotizes them with the nearness of her mystery.

As they struggle to measure up to this danger, don't they make gestures long ago forgotten? And what an astonishing choir the crew makes at this tragic moment!

☆

But, once the storm is over, what will they remember? Won't they once again boast of sailing against the current? Of charting their course against winds and tides? Of overcoming the elements? Of inventing new machines to master them more completely.

And they will laugh at past dangers. And forget. And live on.

And out of the horror they will fashion an epic to captivate the women and children. And take pride in being men. And cover terror in heroism.

That is how the gaps in history are filled. That is how a bright beyond springs out of the shadow.

And do they not inspire terror and respect, as they come back from the grave? Haloed in heroism, do they not attract as much as they repel? Do they not appear to everyone as something more than men? Because they have conquered the sea. And overcome the death which the sea, the double-dealing sea, holds out to the man who advances into her depths. Since they have torn the sea's secret from her. And know everything about her. And know nothing but their terror, by which they become acquainted with a supernatural power.

And move with the assurance of gods, once back in port. Bringing back enough dreams from their trip to last until they set sail again. Enough prestigious appearances not to have to prove their power yet. Enough illusions to live a moment on land.

But sometimes, at night, they are visited by a nightmare. Sometimes, among themselves, they jokingly refer to their fear. Sometimes they recoil at the idea of shipping out next time. They will be forced to leave the shore again, won't they?

And they reassure each other, by saying that death is only met once. What can befall them that they have not already experienced? Are they not bound on the same journey? Crossing well-known territory? Repeating their own actions? Bold are the navigators who go back to sea!

And what is that terror awaiting them in the shadow? That featureless memory of the terrible fight between the slashing breakers and the streaming sails? That peril of water coming from sky and land? And that horror they feel for the might of the sea when she sheds all masks and refuses to be calm, polite, and submissive to the sailors' direction?

And they long for ice. To go further north than north. And to rest on ice. To float in the calm of mirrors. And sleep dry.

If only the sea did not exist. If they could just create her in dreams. If only she did not remain forever, eternally living. And gaping wide in the unattainable depth of her bed.

And they prefer to suffer excessive cold, and harden to the marrow, or wither to the bone in the midday sun, rather than go back to the sea. They prefer to dry up, and die of thirst, rather than run the risk of sinking.

Extreme polar opposites seem more desirable alternatives to them than staying in the middle of the undauntable sea.

To think of the sea from afar, to eye her from a distance, to use her to fashion his highest reveries, to weave his dreams of her, and spread his sails while remaining safe in port, that is the delirium of the sea lover.

After all, it is surely essential to keep what one loves—at a distance? That is what voyagers through eternity claim.

To turn their loves into thought is their highest desire. And gather them all (toutes) together in a single moment. Enclose them in a ring so as to keep them—at a distance. Hold off their end in their return—at a distance. And become, yes, become everything (le tout) —but at a distance.

For everything cannot be touched or embraced at the same time. And the man who gets too close to the other risks merging with it. The man who stays too close to the other risks sinking into it. The man who penetrates the other risks foundering in it. And the other may cease to be his road to becoming what he is.

So get away from the sea. She is far too disturbing. She blurs faces and memories. Her depth is too great. Even when she is limpid, her bed never comes to light. And she is too constantly rained on to become the transparence of dreams. Too restless to be a true mirror.

At a distance: that is where to keep her so as to bind her to his rhythm and to the measure of his will, without his coming back too near to test the reliability of such footbridges. And anything reminiscent of the sea must also be held in the night of sleep.

☆

Out of the sea the superman is reborn, but still he fears to sink under her waters even as he aspires to their vastness. Hermit, tightrope walker or bird, he always keeps away from her great depths.

Between sea and sun, he lives on the earth. And whether those two attract or repel each other in the same element, he still remains between. Life is given him in the (female) one, but he also received it from the other. Cross between plant and ghost. And he can be neither born nor reborn without water, can neither live nor live on without fire and light. But the source of his beginning is always overturned. Because he is walking toward his end. Dwelling in the element necessary to him—the air.

And, in order to be comforted for leaving the (female) one, does he not draw from her his world of dreams and appearances? And, on the road of his recurrence, does he not interpose ice to ground him or sails to carry him back to himself?

## BURNING LAVA YOU CARRY WITHIN YOU

And, within yourself, you no longer stand firm. Within yourself, patiently, violently, after hours of labor, you have unmade the dwelling that was you. That was said to be you.

Moving ceaselessly right and left, up and down, you surveyed that house that was said to be—yours. Crashing into all the boundaries, knocking against all the partitions, and finding far too small the place you had built for yourself, after thousands of years of labor.

So (you) talked to yourself, all alone in that prison: what man has wanted to make well, he still has made to his own measure, the measure of a ressentiment. Evil begins at birth. Now begin again. Return to where the illness begins.

And let that place be empty of all pettiness, of all bitterness and grayness, of all poisonous beasts, of all priests and disciples, of all wise monkeys, of all fear and submission, of all obedience and compassion. . . Make a clean slate of all those feelings that have filled the world with works of revenge. And the world itself, and reason, and the soul, and man, were all of these not created to that standard? Those architectural details must be stripped away. Go beyond, walk further, and break up those certainties with a hammer.

And as you pass through everything again, in all places and times, without truce or respite, you undertook the eradicating cleaning-up of man. And no nook or cranny escaped your anger and your care. Nothing was spared by your love. And you even rendered unto everyone and everything the hatred that they deserved. Which had made them what they were but which they tucked away in their pockets to hatch their little lies, lay their little snares for innocent beasts, put together their little deals.

And from all those little corners, in the twinkling of an eye, you laughed and swept out the goods so laboriously stored! That men, those born shopkeepers, are more attracted to than to life.

You needed to break the spell of goods that were ever more grand and twisted. And what a relentless task! For, if you stopped for even a moment, everything was back in place, more firmly than before.

And how all the captive energy was unleashed in you! And all the sorcery and witchcraft of zeal. What strength you discovered in yourself as you exterminated all that you had believed in so long! All that, through so many lives, had tied you down to idols.

And you laughed at having been so blindly trusting. And burned as you reclaimed the flames once devoted to their cult. And froze to find yourself again in the ring of so much brilliance. A star fallen

53

from the heavens and that knows not what to fecundate with its fires.

☆

And might the eternal recurrence be nothing more than that fragile shell full of lava that you occupy in the end?

But if anything is to be said about it, doesn't that mean breaking the shell and annihilating you? For the fluid cannot be separated from itself that way. Nor is anything in fusion given out drop by drop. And, through giving everything, finds itself nothing.

Unless there be a (female) other of ice who takes nothing and, at least apparently, gives back everything. Whose "yes" declares that she wills nothing except that you should keep everything and that she should mimic that completeness. Perfect as a mirror.

And burning lava you bear within you, like the fragile crust of the world. Everything has melted in the power of your sun. Your love has assimilated all things in its burning flux. And now are you heavy with your will that you have taken back from all things. Now are you a receptacle for unparalleled forces that you would hide within you for fear they might yet be spoiled.

Now you edge forward nervously, or freeze. For don't you risk spilling over if you make the slightest move? And such copious overflow would be a total loss.

And you stay far away from everything and everyone in the midst of the glaciers that help you to keep your burden intact. That environment hardens your shell. Doubles it by their aspect. And, in the last hour, are you not obliged to mimic ice? And look endlessly upon those that are close to the sun and yet remain ice.

This is your highest fortune. And therein have you not achieved your most sublime contrast? Having recapitulated all life in yourself, you become dead so that that moment may be through all eternity.

And now are you explosive, suspended between the moment of its charge and discharge. Awful perspective that, in itself alone, would be enough to paralyze the most intrepid man. Well of life that, by wishing to race through time at least twice, engenders only that part that can be reproduced in accumulation and capitalization. Therefore, not life. That lives all the better as she accumulates less. Burns all excess. Dissolves everything extra in the movement of her becoming.

Why did you not leave all that you had over or in excess to irrigate your flesh? Never will you give birth to a solid body. When you mimic it, you only appear to succeed. And it only outlasts itself beyond death.

Even as you gather all lives together within yourself, yet you will be unable to give life. Give it back, obviously, providing that you give yourself, and the whole of yourself, in your will.

For anyone given drop by drop or by halves always poisons the other and deludes himself about what he is. Each man receives part of the other, and thereby becomes nothingness. Who can keep or lose part, without remaining whole? Tears himself into pieces, and remains nothing. Everything leaks out between the lines of this false division.

And what obstacle tripped you up, you cannot say. Isn't your greatest fear to find a lack of obstacle? Vertigo of the abyss. The risk of melting into something that offers no resistance you can measure up to.

On the edge of this precipice, you seek the secret of your birth and of your death. The strength of your reaction brings you resources to restore you. To wrap you all over again in fallacious reserves and illusory certainties. So you can go far off again, motivated by ressentiment.

Eternal recurrence—the uncommunicable. The time that cannot be spoken without breaking. Since any relation to an outside irreducible to the one already assimilated interrupts the perpetual motion of the cycle.

But within this circle you are lacking what once still sustained your passion. Within that "no" that you make me carry under guise of "yes," aren't you asking me to state that I refuse a share in life with you?

But even if I should say "yes"—that is to say "no"—indefinitely, it will not always have the same effect. Once the ice has formed, you will no longer feel joy and pain coming from beyond.

Between you and me, me and me, you want me to make a dam. You want me to confirm you endlessly in your form so that you can lose yourself over and over again, becoming other while giving a pledge of recurrence.

So is it not a fixed point that you clamor for to continue your work? And if I am chained up in such an alliance, is this a promise of eternal bliss?

## THE CLAMOR OF A NAIVE INSURRECTION

And aren't your powers of deception the result of your impotence, and of the criminal authority you vest in it? As you confuse the real, the act, and their simulacrum within the same, you plunge down into infinite regression.

And (you) know not if your monstrosity is feigned or not. Love or hatred of everything. To act upon or to suffer everything. Strength held in reserve or impossible realization of your highest will. Of your sublimest creation.

And you conspire about everything and nothing, unable to put an end to your crime. Suspended between the yes and the no over a chasm that has not brought its final mystery into the light of day.

And as you want to bring into the world your final thinking, in which all the other thoughts would find their site, you wrap yourself in a cloud of shadow. On the basis of the nonapparent, your thinking develops in the clear light of your day. And the thought rises out of something your day has yet to illumine. And by going down into the abyss to seek higher light, you come back swathed in night. In the place where you intended a new sun to hatch, you spread a chasm of darkness.

Nothing comes into appearing that has not dwelt originally in the natural element. That has not first taken root in an environment that nourished it undisturbed by any gaze. Shielded from the unveiling of any fixed form.

Thus your first night, and a more ancient one than any your day has produced or dreamed of. Or your reason either. Or your language. Thus your ultimate recurrence, and one still less likely to be outdone than the reverse side of your discourse. Your madness.

Forever you lose hold of the place where you take body. And to repeat your own birth is simply impossible. And by wishing for it, you choose to die. Finding again that dark home where you began to be once upon a time. Once and for all.

That event does not happen twice. That necessity and that chance, horrendous and wonderful as they are in the blind term of their meeting.

And, as you enter into the eternity of your recurrence, you cut yourself off from that unique occasion when you received life. All powerful, perhaps, for a fleeting moment; until the thread breaks that connected you to the earth. Then begins the decline.

Even as you imagined, for a fleeting moment, that within you you could recapitulate any other, the dizzy madness of forging such a monstrous identity heralds your end. The other and you can be interminably exchanged only in appearances. And the appearance that detaches itself from the life where it had taken place gradually loses hold on life. And such transparency only lights the way for a time. And anyone who seeks to sustain himself by means of the transparency he sees as the greatest power will fail.

And perhaps a god gets to such a height. But dead.

So wasn't it better to remain a cross between plant and ghost? And give to at least one part of yourself: earth, water, air, and sun? Until you are able to embrace yourself with the other in all those elements.

And have you forgotten the love your god had for plants? Surely it is a sign of decline when you want only artificial flowers.

And did your idol not come from the bottom of the sea? Did it not habitually return there at times of greatest peril? Did it not find its survival in the sea?

But never appeared definitively. Destiny never took on a single face. And imitating that was the impossible part of your dream. How is one to mimic something that has no identity? That is fixed in no form. Cannot be encompassed. Eluding capture and catalog, except for the mask—death.

And in the end have you not subjected your god to a fate that you did not intend? Forgotten that he enjoyed good wine and women more than images. And reduced to a cipher the song of his music.

☆

And so many shadows still sleep in the cradle of the deep. How much silence still rests deep down below!

And what rustlings arise from everything that grows underground. And what impatience to live in everything held back from blossoming. A call to birth that rages at the delay it must suffer as you sit down to consult your language and assign it a name!

And while you are terrified of chasms and paralyzed by lightning, you cannot hear the clamor of that naive insurrection.

And you delight in this new morning that lights up your setting. Doesn't this make you want to move on?

But let the sea cover over the marks you still inscribe on your tables of exile! And waves crash over your last hour's whims. And the sun sets fire to your sheets, melts your wax, and metal shells and all the machines for reproducing your sovereign edicts. And the winds sweep away those traces of laws laid down in loneliness.

If only they could at the same time carry your soul away in the merry whirlwind of their breath! And if the sand could spread its banks over your countless footsteps and erase the tracks that always return to the same point, and embrace nothing but places of extradition.

Yes, let all the elements finally conspire against the procedures you follow in only dwelling far away in the land of dreams. And you would remember that the elements still originate outside your language. And that within language, with it, next to it, you keep interposing yourself, as if language were the only thing that existed. And that the sea, sun, air, and earth you talk about were already shrunk to fit that immortal language! And that you are dying of immortality.

And if your truths or appearances or simulacra have already been fished out in such a net, what do these differences matter! They arise out of a bottomless pit of life. And constitute always a golden prison where you decline and carry everything with you to ruin.

And (I) would rather live in a seaweed hollow than in your gleaming palaces. And roll in the grass than in your ice fields. And drench myself over and over again in sea and shower, rather than be clean and polished so that I can shine in your sun's brilliance. And (I) shall rather drink morning dew than your venerable lore. Too often (I) have absorbed paralyzing venom from your words. Have too often woken from the intoxication of such a drink to find myself between a flashing star and a gravestone, between a burning torch and the shallow waters left behind by the tide. Thrown aside or else left standing as you switch back and forth, (I) can no longer manage to find the song of my becoming. Far from that movement wherein my lips unendingly savor the taste of life.

And I shall escape a mask custom-made to beguile you. For smothering myself in such vain show repels me. And (I) will not abet you in your crimes or in your dying. And (I) prefer to keep my living skin so that, at any time to come, I may share it. And better unmask than mask again what is calling out to be born.

And so many faces are still to come that I want to select none of them. Pick none of them out as the best and most beautiful. To appear always other, that is my pleasure. And to stop being born only when it is time to die.

For if someone wears a mask, is he not trying to hide the total absence of a face? To cover over the desertion of his body? To lure into the abyss one who is deceived by the mere appearance of life? And to feed on innocent prey so as to gain new strength, pursue one's plans for destruction, and taste the rapture of revenge upon the unforeseen and imponderable surge of life. That can never be fixed in any definitive form.

For if someone takes a mask he is, obviously, diverging from one established identity. But is arrested in the figure of one of them (elles). Which can be monstruous, or parodic. Arresting the movement of becoming, withholding it from appearing. Not letting it be seen as it metamorphoses. And endlessly holding itself back from being born behind that envelope of artifice. Still mimicking the gestation of nature, even while annihilating it? Nature cannot be imitated. The mobility of her growth is never fixed in a single form that can serve as template. And is nature's creation not destroyed when one of her moments is taken out and recreated as permanence?

And how revolting for the lovers who close and touch is that vain show! A death contact that repels and keeps ever at a distance.

## AN ABYSSAL FORGETFULNESS

So, since the bottom has never been sounded, all realities and all truths about it remain on the level of superficial appearances. They move away from the bottom and muddy it with the material they have borrowed from it. That which has never been plumbed still hides in a night far deeper than your day has imagined.

And anyone who wants to cut through those layers that prevent the bottom from appearing risks coming upon a great silence and an abyssal forgetfulness. Risks entering that sleep and that dream which weave the fabric of the world, its cycles, and revolutions. Risks moving forward lucidly, blindly, in search of something he left on the far side of any boundary.

But anything brought back from that perilous adventure is surely dead to the gaze of the moment? Icebergs and cliffs rear up that had already been annihilated as far as movements of becoming go. And how is one to come back alive from a voyage which alternates between propulsive speed into what is apparently still empty and the inertia of dead weights?

And everything you conceive, you believe can be brought into being. But if the bottom that underlies appearing escapes you, how can it be given existence?

Thus your highest creations presuppose a crime. Whether actually perpetrated or not doesn't matter! At the bottom of each of your acts lies a murder that undermines them.

And what have you killed that pursues you with such endless ghosts, horror, and trembling? Something that has still to see the light of day for you? Something that still stands apart, where you cannot overcome it, overpower it, fly over it, survive it?

"So, I have not killed anything?"

Yes you have. Before coming into the light, life is already living. It is germinating long before it responds to your sun's rays.

And, obviously, behind every appearance hides an infinite number of others. But, behind all appearances, there remains an irreducible life that cannot be captured by appearance. Unless it withers away.

And to see and hear this as merely the defensive secret of some essence whose resistance must be broken, here is indeed the dream of a late-comer!

So your perpetual genesis will be the perpetuation of a crime committed. A dream envelope with which, indefinitely, you cover over all that was fomenting in the crypt. The burial, from the outset, of something that will never shine in the splendor of your noon.

And you mimic nature even as you destroy the original of her work. That belongs to no artist. And remains without a model.

And your land teems with masks and monsters. Your dawn harbors degeneracy and decline if you persist in giving birth in ways out of step with a virgin nature that knows not man. If you refuse to wed that other (woman) as a stranger, and to share with her without either wanting or being able to possess her.

And if you ask her to mimic herself within you and thereby double the spectacle you present, does this amount to asking her to proclaim that destroying nature is the highest act of fidelity we can offer nature? Given that nature never recapitulates herself, never closes over the life or the death she gives out, but allows each to happen when the hour strikes.

By wishing to put your becoming into a circle, aren't you anticipating some murderous triumph over forces that are given freely, according to a game of chance and necessity, forces that cannot be contained or held back. Or mastered. Unless they wither away because they did not see any light at that moment when the sap was determined on bloom. Neither later nor earlier. Neither yesterday

61

nor tomorrow, when it must be today. And on this occasion, this single occasion. That can never be repeated.

And this is what the lover of life wants, is it not: to take from her that source that is inaccessible in its mystery? Since he can only give at given intervals, and according to his will. Even if he does not want to.

## THE DESERT IS GROWING

Between your will and your body, the river no longer circulates. The lava does not flow from the (male) one to the other, from the other to one, without a break.

And the (male) one always arrives too early or too late or not at all at the event that is allotted to the other. And an infernal dance is set up by those discordant rhythms that allow no place for harmony. And you are obliged to give up the other to live the (male) one, and the one to live the other. And to jump from one fragment to another. Torn on both sides.

Enigmatic rubble that rises again out of construction framed from time immemorial with the forces of revenge. And their forgetfulness.

And don't you get your pleasure (jouir) out of flying from the one to the other, flying from the one to the other and the other to the one, as if from a supreme triumph? Don't you in the end want to find the music of the whole beneath the continents you cut up into secular units? Or is your game to exaggerate that decomposition? Both? And what if you had to make a choice? What if both at the same time amounted to a decision in favor of the (male) one? If the terms of your contradictions were posed in such a way that, if you strain them further, you bring down that awful destruction you do not wish for? If your oppositions already implied refusing? Rejecting your birth? Setting outside your circle the body in which you have had place? Exile from the place where you have had place?

As you fly over the map with your eagle's eye. The eye of a bird of prey soaring above the world that feeds him? And swooping down only to take the blood of others. Returning, of course, to the proud heights to digest his prey!

But summits that live on the life of others must necessarily be subject to deep depressions, must they not? That find bliss in the lack of their own sustenance.

And if one were to live in one's own element, and not abandon one's nature and soar to such a height, might this not herald a greater rapture? If you were to break your "no" instead of breaking yourself? And to recast your kingdom of exile instead of reigning in sovereignty there as master of the end of the world. In the emanation of dreams cradled in the illusion that the lack created is source and sign of higher good fortune.

These are the last priests—the scientists who preach famine. Degenerate men who still barely survive on the smoke from the sacrifices of others. And who take pride in being more than men, since they have climbed to such heights. And gaze on the desert as proof of their power.

Waiting for the epiphany of some new god. Some as yet unfamiliar incarnation of an idol in whom to hail the future of their destiny.

And instead they watch the machines multiply that push them little by little beyond the limits of their nature. And they are sent back to their mountain tops, while the machines progressively populate the earth. Soon engendering man as their epiphenomenon.

And they are also on the lookout for those who, on all fours or crawling, mimic the still innocent beasts in order to discover their secret path to wisdom. The desert is growing. Woe to whoever. . .

Acquired knowledge. One has to get back to the birth of evil. And reevaluate every measurement and division.

And if one casts out of the self anything that might be depth, and if one wishes only for appearances, doesn't this amount, in the end, to letting go of life? Becoming a ghost? And coming back to haunt solid realities since they are the only things that refuse to vanish into thin air? That still remind you of existing.

But, in that case, isn't one colliding with corpses? Matter artificially deprived of all movement. Mortal remains already sunk into inertia.

And who has created such distance between him and himself, between body and soul, that he is now obliged to sail between two dead things and keep looking for the way to ensure the return of the female one (l'une) into the other? And how can footbridges be built between the female one and the other?

And by wanting to span that gap, does he not in fact cast discord down into the pit of infinite regression? Does he not set the dead so far aside that the event leading to their brutal isolation and even starvation is forgotten?

And where is life to find a way, if death is at birth? And how is the riddle to be solved that opens up that memoryless crypt?

Surely, emphasizing rupture in this way is a kind of revenge. Incapable of bringing yourself into the world, you hated the one that gave you life, didn't you? And you reduced to nothing that power that holds aloof from your art? And made death out of native life.

And if anything comes near you for some gift or other, you paralyze it. Don't you love life? Don't you want to become life itself? Eternal life? To the nature that still sustains you, isn't your response: this time, my turn to choose?

You go off to meditate. You assimilate as you will. You reject the rest as a burden. Or earthly attraction? And you reappear, as a ghost. According to refraction or diffraction, in this shape or another. In this (male) shape and the other. Multiple, yet broken. And, as a living being, unable to overcome the need to share.

And you go back to the beginning of this operation ceaselessly. Nostalgic for a very ancient past. If you were to recreate the whole in one single moment, would you not avoid separation?

Faster and faster you go back to the beginning, to get a jump on your birth. That hole and that weight that are recalled in soul and body? And you flee from the one and the other, and run after the one and the other. And spin around very quickly in order to melt and recast them otherwise. Into a (male) one.

And again and yet again the whole disintegrates and fragments. The (male) one is lost, also the (female) other. The ring is broken. The rapture gone. Disenchantment reappears.

☆

Still you have not begun to live. Now start again. (The) evil begins at birth.

Birth. La naissance. La naissance? La? Naissance? And what if that (ça) didn't mean anything in your language? If that/the id meant nothing, in your language?
Birth? An abstract phenomenon assumed by anyone coming into existence. A dead skin imperceptibly wrapping anyone that has just come into appearing. A proper noun permanently covering over anyone who enters into his becoming. A deceit to be worn through every change. An airy hiding place that encircles all becoming in its veil.

And how can one claim to grow endlessly on the near side and the far side of those native surroundings? And how much shrieking and writhing is needed to rid oneself of such originary inhumation.

(The) evil begins at birth—the birth of your language. You have to go farther back than the point where you saw the light of day. To set your coming into daylight within this language-malady, does that not already mean acceding in your decline? Believing that what gives you life is an obstacle to life? And wanting life to be engendered from a language-body alone?

So here is your sun in his universe of forces, rays, and signs of different intensities. Giving new meaning to every living thing. But where does it get the matter for combustion? Doesn't the sun endlessly take back as much as it gives, in order to illumine? And how does it decide on its turn? And what place does the sun drink from before climbing up into the heavens? And is that enough? Is the sun not endlessly attracted by its setting?

And what becomes of alternating white and black horizons, borders of days and nights, transparency of mask and nesting which is yet to appear, in that transmutation beyond the envelope in which life is offered for the first time? Doesn't this imply a change of skins that cannot happen without death? The abandon of the (female) one believed to be a sepulcher in favor of the other that leads you (vous) into nothingness?
The essential thing being—to impose your will. Without sharing.

65

And whether you shiver or burn, that is your fortune as long as you think you are master of these dangers, and assume you can overcome them one day.

But the evil begins at birth. He who mistakes his skin when coming into the world will indefinitely seek the arrival in port.


## ADVERSITY BY CHANCE

And finally, in your search for a rival who can match up to you, aren't you really seeking to break the mirror created by ressentiment? Isn't the urge to fight on equal terms your last effort to overcome the fight of pro and con that rages within you? To excel in this way, aren't you obliged to contest energy of like intensity? And isn't your worst enemy the man who refuses to fight that way and comes to you unarmed? Offering you only abyss and swamp into which the sharpest of your blades sinks. Your hatred back in those shallow waters you thought you had left behind you forever, o superman!

So let us hope someone like yourself turns up to pull you out of the mud! Someone other, and yet like, a faithful mirror to help you cross back through the layers of those great depths. Dragging you once again out of the whole where you lived before you rose so high.

And what a struggle that impossible choice wages within you! To be or not to be the only one, isn't that still your dilemma? And you have invented no grammar other than the one that creates the gods —that makes you god. And no other love but war to the death against everything that surrounds you and holds you back from climbing to that supreme illusion.

The danger of immersion in primary matter endlessly feeds your anguish, your forgetfulness, and your death. Your tomb, ever close at hand.

And doesn't your will to survive endlessly plan to open up new paths, a new escape route, a new sky on this earth? To pierce holes that let you breathe, move about, and fly. And you thrust back to the edges of the place you now occupy the thing that always threatens to engulf you—filling your nose, your mouth, your eyes, your ears with immemorial waters.

And (you) never resolve this question, pushing it back to the periphery of what you consider to be the livable world. And (you) find yourself a captive in a prison universe. Horizon, house, body or soul closed upon themselves. Surviving, no doubt. But stopped dead in your becoming.

And what thoughts have you not had about the fluid world you once inhabited? Sending it back to the bottom or hardening it to make a shell that nothing can leak through.

And should you overflow and let your waters flow into the sea, where are the children born to you out of such generosity? Where, your underwater creations?

And who is it that you must overcome? Who brought you into the light of day? Was it earth and sea that gave you birth, like one of their blossoms, that tenderly leave you to be nourished by the living element around you? In the midst of what gives you power?

Or was it—yourself when you passed by earlier? And don't you confuse the two, annihilating the (female) one because you wish to overcome the other? Circling endlessly around the point where that mystery moved into the abyss—of the separation from her, from yourself.

Where does difference begin? Where is it (elle)? Where am I? And how can one face something that hides from appearing? How can one master that dark place where you find birth? Where you begin to be.

And by wanting to reduce that past time in which your strength is deep frozen, aren't you destroying the time in which you receive it? From which still living strength flows.

Endlessly, you turn back to that enigmatic question, but you never go on, you leave it still in the dark: who is she? who am I? How is that difference marked? Outside the struggle to the death with yourself-already-same (avec toi déjà même). With the other you have already created for yourself as a possible adversary in your world.

To begin, and again begin, each act with a duel, isn't this a dream of measuring your power? But in this face-to-face combat between likes, she whom you want to overcome has already disappeared. Your strength is already rated according to its power as mirage. Already you fight your visions, ghosts, and simulacra of every type. Already you forget the hatred that bends what you call the living to your will—to overcome life.

A worthy opponent? Are you calling for the destruction of the power of the mirror? Taking stock of your hatred, and going beyond it? Estimating the power of your ressentiment and, by loosing such energy, heralding a future other than the time of revenge?

Or: are you gathering everything that is man together, and, by recapitulating in him all becoming, creating him as more man than he ever was in the past. Redoubling, beneath his footsteps, in a perfect circle, the ground of an origin that he gives himself. God at last.

☆

Opponent? But, insofar as he reflects the shows you put on, is it possible such an opponent might occur? Only adversity comes into the world, perchance.

A chance happening that defies calculation? Like a storm cloud that condenses tattered wisps of material resistance. Shadows of bodies masking the limpid dryness of the air. Remains of incarnations that still remain under the sun and flit randomly out to block the purity of the light.

And how is one to take a position against such an enemy? Or flee that impalpable dilution of revenge that fills the atmosphere and does not spare you according to the weather.

A duel? A luxury of the past. Where can you find a body to touch, wound, run through, in your era? And if by chance such a body turns up, isn't it already bloodless?

But, apart from this encounter, what force field you are still endlessly obliged to cross in order to survive! And whereas some are already dead, and some still living, they all wander outside their mortals' skins. Beyond any face, and without countenance, they fill the air with their threat of death.

And before you have even noticed the enemy appear, you will be felled by a blow from an imperceptible weapon. That is the will of your fortune, you the sublime of the last day.

## MOURNING IN LABYRINTHS

The eternal recurrence—what is that but the will to recapitulate all projects within yourself? To undo the place where all projections ought to converge? Since their term provides them with a good direction. Snatching his ultimate power, and secret, from some God. Giving your will back to the multiple and to the instant of its play.

But, when you killed the Other, didn't you thereby also eliminate every other? What hideous confusion! Stripping yourself of any basis for inscribing, setting out, and making fruitful your urges, flights, and productions. Except for—blank pages, representations, roles, masks . . . ? By demanding that something that is already spectacular should be redoubled, aren't you suppressing the as yet imperceptible effects of your intentions? Surging up necessarily from a circle in order to return to yourself.

For, in the other, you are changed. Become other, and without recurrence. It is up to her to perpetuate your becoming, to give it back to you or not, variously deformed. A trace of your passage into her leaves a mark, in the flesh. That forever escapes you.

That trace, that gift—aren't you pondering ways to get them back? Reincorporate, reassimilate them into yourself? Use all the shapes in which you have had or will have place to make a becoming other for yourself alone. The becoming of a (male)-self-same (d'un même).

And if you wanted to lose one of your given identities, that would be fine! But not the unique identity of a becoming. Of a becoming same. Your single and eternal necessity.

In that necessity any (male) other assures you of a movement that is always other and always same. Females or males (elles ou ils) forced in their differences or diversity to obey your cycle: kept evenly spaced around a center where they return to the same. Your becoming is attracted by or into them, and risks being lost there. Unless, as it circles around the object or the aim of its attraction, it turns back into the same.

Like a snake that endlessly enfolds the one on the edge formed or projected by its desire. Or a sun, whose rays might conceivably bring

69

back to their focus the illumination of all things. Or the man who brings back into himself the ecstasies of his will, and projects his strength, his tension, his energy, his seed . . . only so that he can repossess the effects of those gifts and find fresh nourishment, and new growth in them. A new birth, or a survival.

That last thought, you are unable to express.

—For expressing it might mean, might it not, to risk it entering into the becoming other of the other—unless it were a mirror other (une autre de glace). Might mean abandoning your luck to the keeping of the other. Opening the circle of recurrence. The play of chance and necessity. And the conquest of the random in the perpetual movement of becoming. Giving it at least two poles. Which undoes the permanence of the identical.

—For expressing it might mean, might it not, breaking the ring in which you are now standing (back). The alliance of a successful idealism? But once you have stripped the idea of matter, form, substance, end, power . . . so that you can melt them down and recast them otherwise, then you have lost all communicable stability. Nothing remains for you to show, demonstrate, signify, exchange, coin . . . at a distance. Except yourself? Held fast in your creation, you produce yourself as a creation. Are you transfigured in it? The other has given you the distance necessary for the operation. But if, here and now, the other is not available to you, you lose both yourself and her in that same distance. And you have nothing left, not simulation, not mask, not interpretation, to use as procedures to play off between chaos and appearances. You have become a mask and can no longer change it. Mask of the man cut off from his continuous resource in the living. Frozen by your language into an attitude, an unchangeable, paralytic character part, whose buffoon, whose puppet you are, at this last hour.

Incarnating your idea. Thus placing yourself at a distance but no longer capable of undoing that pose. Creation-creature of your thought. Eternally offered up as a show for your descendants.

—For expressing it implied the need for means and instruments of translation. And your language was lacking in the processes and mediations of such a reality, wasn't it? Every time you want to speak, to mean, don't you fail? Proclaiming the event, but not managing to put the unsaid into words.

Do you really want to do so? Wouldn't your will break if you willed it to make an appearance outside of this specific moment? By covering yourself with a mask, and remaining forever still, aren't you signifying that any gesture, any mimicry, from that point, risks annihilating the pose thus discovered—by chance and necessity. That has been sculpted by eternity. Having returned the chisel to Apollo, conqueror of Dionysos, after all the famous raving and up-heaval.

When you gave precedence to interpretation over the movement of life, didn't you thereby choose this fate?

—For expressing it has been attempted, hasn't it? After all. Out of fear? Refusal of such a terrible day of reckoning? But who was able or willing to hear you? Was there a potential interlocutor for such a thought? Or only a spectator? Or a spectatrix?

Was she able, was she willing to hear you? Or look upon you? Did she even command power and will in the place where you used to take her? Were you not making an appeal she was doubly and triply incapable of receiving? To locate herself outside two histories: yours, hers, and the relations between them. In order to admire and repro-duce the realization, successfully executed in its final designs, of your becoming. As she cast off all the veils in which she was hidden and imprisoned, she had yet to sustain that destiny which forever set you apart from her, maintaining the (male) one and the other at a definitive distance.

Unless once again she agrees to submit to her role, returning anew into your life, as the fixed center-point and also the outside, keeping up the movement of your cycle. Thus parted from her birth, her growth, the unfolding of her becoming, her life. Energy at the dis-posal of the becoming of a (male) same. Was this not the death plot which cannot hold beyond the specific instant?

Was it left to her to interpret? To try to undo the work in its last pose? To invent a different relation to the same and the other? That deconcentrates the circle and permits an as yet unencountered play in the relationship? Other music, other graphics, other plastic art of hymen—and within language too.

That was not your request. And, no doubt, you would not have wished it. This chance of a meeting of two necessities in a new alliance has not taken place. If the effects of history were overcome, did this not imply that you proposed yourself as indispensable pro-logue to an other future? That allowed the completed figure of man's

desire to be heard, or seen The work of his solitary will. The achievement, perhaps, of his highest ressentiment toward whoever resists—
irreducibly other.

For expressing it surely entailed going beyond the projective
mechanism by playing it over, and playing around with it. But, once
their foundation has been taken away, the projections come back to
you. You inhabit them, they inhabit you. There is a return to you
and within you of something that finds no place to settle—investing,
cathecting yourself.

So you become the Crucified One. Him whom you projected-
rejected out of yourself, by willing yourself to be Dionysos. This last,
and constant, fight inside your world involves the ebbing back upon
you of the object of your ressentiment, at least as it is perceived.
Giving up, according to your will, the spirit of revenge, you live that
ultimate contradiction of being both that will and its contrary: both
murderer and victim.

And, as an end, you serve as foundation for the images, the figure,
the role, that you unremittingly laid down in your active project.
Having passively become the mask of Christ. The realization of your
destiny?

But were Dionysos and the Crucified One really different? Did
they not, secretly, have the same birth within your universe? If so,
you would have engaged and sought to overcome only a sham phony
contradiction—one created by a subjective error. The game would
stop for lack of contestants. Upon the discovery that the two actors
were of the same gender and type, perhaps? You would have failed
to search far enough or deep enough to find the source of your
antagonisms. And the origin of your ressentiment.

—For expressing it, in what way? Were you not immersed in the
other? A (male) other whose identity and language you did not know.
An other that was—dumb? Between the character you have wrapped
yourself in and the speeches you have been making, a great gap has
opened up. That leaves you, you also, deprived of language. And
there's no question any more of pretense, parody, acting: you are
that character. You shriek and writhe, freed by the uncontrollable
rupture, the irrecoverable abyss, between your world of yesterday
and the world surrounding you today. Which world? And how to
express it? You meet Ariadne or Diotima or. . . You want to marry
her. To chain her to your side, as guardian of your hearth, so that

your work can be accomplished. She refuses. Stresses her freedom in the face of your will. You try to find your balance again, fail. Except in the eternal recurrence that creates an autological movement that cannot be reopened. By giving yourself up wholly to a center in which the other has no role except as counterweight or balance arm between you and yourself, you cannot get out of the circle. You die at that moment, the work being perfect—remains to live on.

The limit traced in this way is achieved by and against her. It is a closure that reacts to the effects of her "no." And to what you fail to decathect of her. Without being able to interpret her. Lost as you are in a labyrinth. For the first time, you measure yourself up against a will of equal strength, yet different from your own, and you are lost.

☆

She is your labyrinth, you are hers. A path from you to yourself is lost in her, and from her to herself is lost in you. And if one looks only for a play of mirrors in all this, does one not create the abyss? Looking only for attractions to return into the first and only dwelling, does one not hollow out the abyss?

Unless difference is affirmed, the inclusion of you in her, and her in you, spins off into a labyrinthine mourning for desire or for will inside you both (vous) and between you both.

And, forever covered over or possessed by your projections, she will give them back to you as things neither she nor you want, and in which you do not recognize your will. Beyond the horizon you have opened up, she will offer you that in which she still lives and that your day has not even imagined. And yet, the multiple layers of veil and disguise are hiding such depth. Are calling on you to drop the mask and stop the show so that you may marry and make merry (faire la noce) at last—that is not your fortune!

# VEILED LIPS

To write that "from the very first nothing is more foreign . . . to woman than truth," and then that "her great art is falsehood, her chief concern is appearance and beauty" (*Beyond Good and Evil*, p. 232)* is surely to say the same thing twice, with the exception that one word has been forgotten the second time, the word *foreign*.

Neither falsehood nor appearance and beauty are "foreign" to truth. They are proper to it, if not its accessories and its underside. And the opposite remains caught up in the same. It grounds the economy—or echonomy—of sameness. With a flip of the coin, it forms the basis for its representations. Foreign, for its part, beckoned toward an outside. But it was *forgotten*.

Mimesis is not to be outflanked this way. Certainly not by "woman"— double. Her only function is to go along with the movement, clothing it well or badly, but letting it develop freely, undistorted. By "femininity" least of all.

But woman? Is not to be reduced to mere femininity. Or to falsehood, or appearance or beauty. Short of staying out of it, (idem, p. 232)† and projecting at (from) a distance that other of the self to which truth is, from the outset, hostile: falsehood, as well as beauty and appearance, . . . Although femaleness has taken it/them as part of her forms, although she cannot do without it/them if she is to pass for what is: the truth.

This operation also will be attributed to woman. Or is it to femininity? As a preparation for "woman." Who may be said to play with it as with a setting, framing, mounting, glazing. Until the time

*Quotations from Nietzche's works are made from the following translations: *Beyond Good and Evil*, in *Basic Writings of Nietzsche*, translated by Walter Kaufman (Random House, Modern Library Giant, 1968); *The Gay Science, with a Prelude in Rhymes and an Appendix of Songs*, translated with a commentary by Walter Kaufman (Random House, Vintage Books, 1974); *The Birth of Tragedy*, translated by Francis Golfing (Doubleday Anchor Books, 1956); *The Twilight of the Idols* in *The Portable Nietzsche*, edited and translated by Walter Kaufman (Penguin Books, 1954); *Daybreak*, translated by R. J. Hollingdale (Cambridge University Press, 1982).—Tr.
†In the French translation, "rester entre soi."—Tr.

she? gets out? If in fact she ever plays. But so many things are attributed to whoever remains foreign to self-definition. Who risks —the abyss. If that stays a little while, without return to the same.

Hence the comedy of the other. Another aspect of its performance that truth does not always appreciate: the comic. To attribute this to the other is once again to clothe it in a mask, but meanwhile reserve the right to make use of it from time to time. To take back, when the moment or the desire demands, something that is never given except as a loan. That can therefore be used freely, without incurring any debt. It was only held in trust.

The problems arise when the body by which this guarantee of dissimulation is ensured is in some way reactive. As is the case with "our hysterical little women," for example, It is as well not to count on them for that affirmative dissimulation which seduces and plays the truth. Their feeling of ressentiment spoils "our" appearances.

How can one recognize oneself in their writhings and grimaces without being repelled? These are scarcely even caricatures of a work of art. When you come right down to it, it's phony, false, fake, deceptive, etc. And undisguisedly so.

Mastery asserts itself by skirting such a naked obscenity. A disgrace to the whole theater of representation. Irreducible contortion of a nature mimicking the residue of a properly staged mimicry. Why do women, our women, lie so poorly?

And how is one to get through that absence of veils: horror. Immodest display of the mummified remains of the Dionysiac. Not those/its excesses overflowing in the Apollonian festival, but that extra element from before—and from "the fraternal union of the two deities" (*Birth of Tragedy*, p. 21)—that suffers from being cut into pieces by individuation even though it has never known completeness. Dispersal into fragments that do not tear apart unity, and can therefore never be put back together.

Except in the phantasy of the other. Of the same. Its veil(s). And what "operation" will cut through that cloth—phantasy? The "production" of another phantasy? Another phantasy of the other? Attributed to the other? Of the same. Male/female in its depth/superficiality according to the way they want to deck it out. So that the inside or the outside can be laid down or laid away in it. According to the pleasure or the pain that is wished for, the death wish that will be celebrated, at one moment in history.

Thus, if error becomes the "truth" of pleasure, the "idea" becomes woman. Woman becomes the possibility of a "different" idea, which amounts to a store of strength. "The eternal feminine" moves away, goes into exile in another representation: that will find pathos in the crucifixion of Christ, that scion of Dionysos.

"(Progress of the idea: it becomes more subtle, insidious, incomprehensible—it *becomes female,* it becomes Christian.)" ("How the 'True World' Finally Became a Fable. The History of an Error," in *The Twilight of the Idols.*) This point is made with special emphasis by being tucked away—perhaps necessarily here?—behind brackets. One kind of distancing that pins down the feminine in a display. Woman, even Christ, would merely serve as dummies to be clothed in the finery needed to capture the pleasure of the idea. When she was too cold, she was boring; when too synonymous with being, she no longer left any place for the perceptible; too theoretical, she neutralized even the *pathos* of death. . . Something red was lacking, a hint of blood and guts to revive the will, and restore its strength. A wound. Which however will only be opened up in its representation from within that extra setting: the brackets.

The articulation of two repetitions, of two different circles around the re-beginning, isn't this always, and still, the way a sign is made? And is "woman"—plus femininity—anything but that residue of ideas that, once it has been doubly wrapped up, serves to capture doing as sign?

This may be read as: she gives herself out to be: what she is not.* This operation would be implied in the game of the other. Of the same. Interpreted in this way, she stakes him in a new game without his needing to borrow from the kitty. And therefore go into debt, risk losing. Mastery. Which the other (of the same) threatens him with. From afar, given the way he is placed at a distance by the economy of truth.

How to defend oneself from an adversary who is so subtly absent? The danger is dizzying in its deceit. How to finance the death of one's other? Since one is master only at that price, which is not even really paid. By oneself. And the other, in its mirage, threatens only by a recall of what one has secretly confided to its care: this deposit of death. That the master needed. But not for self.

And if he once had made the tour of his properties, and found

* In the French, "elle se donne pour."—Tr.

everything to be mortal, how could the other fail to send him back this reflection? He still had one chance: not to mix up and homogenize castration (theoretical construct) and castrating (act of gelding). Not to forget that marks and masks are different in their relations with signs. The absolute of mastery injures itself thereby, deprives itself only of the whole. Not of life: of pleasure, of pain. Nor of play, or appearance. Because to play all on one's own? . . .

Castration stems/sublates from the giving of the self into the making the self "out to be." From doing as sign. Or else operates in an undecidable zone between truth, "truth," and appearances. That castration would claim to arbitrate, even while playing it, playing with it, making sport of it. Scheming, seductive, not foreign to the processes of affirmation and dissimulation—which will nonetheless be held at bay. Not foreign, of course, to reaction.

The femininity of woman, that would be her other, which amounts to the same. It would even at times slightly hint at the-act-of-castrating, but only in a scientific perspective. Now science . . . Freud/Nietzsche. It is preferable to move on to art where one can play with castration better. Everything fits in. For example: maternity-femininity-prostitution. Even matter: they're the same. And appearance, forms, masks, veils—the whole paraphernalia of beauty. And if beauty is to be intensely perceived, differences are essential, it seems? Even ugliness, and the suspension between the one and the other.

Castration? Wasn't that, precisely, the gesture of repetition which gave the key to the whole stage set by the same? And therefore gave it some play, gave the game the possibility: to be played. In the second or third degree: the Apollonian dream, the Socratic truth, the simulacrum (both of them within a certain indifference, a repeat that suspends the gash between them, covers the [female] one and the other and yet never really does so, still adhering to a belief in difference, if only to play with it).

Castration would be merely some simulacrum—with nothing added on—unless the other has nothing, and is not lent what she doesn't have, what she would have been allowed only to take care of. So that she can threaten, by playing or not playing according to the charge she has been invested with—of castration. Castration might be interpreted as a simulacrum used to frighten oneself, and therefore as the source of pleasure in continuing the game.

For example? To simulate depth in the guise of the bigger or the smaller. To bring erection and limpness into the game of castration. And the other into the same: a comparison between the bigger and the smaller, the harder and the softer, etc., until it becomes impossible to evaluate anything except in terms of *less* and *more*.

A repetition, then, with signs. Which are now agreed to be simulated in part, with which there will be a generalization of the giving oneself out to be: that which is not. The economy-echonomy of what is is thereby affected. Not necessarily the mastery. Perhaps by admitting the part played by illusion, by claiming it openly, airing it publicly, one is cleared of the burden of a secret, the guilt of concealment, of the pure and simple assurance of being adequate to mastery. Not by losing. Especially if the scenario is now presumed to be *general*. Including this residue: the other would threaten castration. The other? Of the same? If castration means the same thing as: kill him, if it is equivalent to death, then the other is equivalent to the same. Or else perpetuates the alternation of everything and nothing. Fulfilling the master's desire. Which he can dress up differently, according to the historical moment.

Given up more and more to "foreignness" now that castration has been taken over by the master's desire, the-act-of-castrating recircumscribes the practice of the game from some kind of outside. But it is forgotten in castration.

Or, sometimes, circumcision. Now the Jewish operation, despite what is cut away, lies in the realm of the sign. What is cut away is only cut away in order to make a sign. It is "true" that it is also in the realm of the body. But almost the reverse of castrating, this excision is what marks the body's entry into the world of signs.

And that will make a stain, a spot. No one is supposed to notice the opening onto the stage of sameness. Otherwise that unfortunate, that disconcerting change would have to be paid for, everywhere, by everybody. Therefore it has to be "repeated," so that it can be erased, forgotten, put back in the pack. All of which is no longer possible without suppressing the whole of the body. And when horror is law, the result is exile, death. The stage is set outside-inside for the theater of representation.

Unless the Jew agrees to take on the actor's role? As an affirmative doubling of his operation, just for laughs. Which (he believes? they believe?) he can allow himself since he has already paid for it.

"What good actor today is *not*—a Jew? The Jew as a born 'man of letters,' as the true master of the European press, also exercises his power by virtue of his histrionic gifts; for the man of letters is essentially an actor. He plays the 'expert,' the 'specialist' " (*The Gay Science*, p. 361).

And rightly so, moreover: circumcision attests to a specialist's expertise in the field of signs. Should the rest of the stage be transformed into a protesting chorus, in the name of castration no less, that changes, in fact, nothing. The spot left by the Jew is still there. To make him play it over again as a simulacrum is worth more. Provided he is made to pass as other. And without a veil? The thing taken from him was (only) a blind. Though a necessary one. His role will therefore be to enact dissimulation.

> Finally *women*. Reflect on the whole history of women: do they not *have* to be first of all and above all else actresses? Listen to physicians who have hypnotized women; finally, love them—let yourself be 'hypnotized' by them! What is always the end result? That they 'put something on' even when they take off everything. Woman is so artistic . . . (*The Gay Science*, p. 361)*

"Do they not *have* to be"/"histrionic gifts"; effect of castrating/effect of circumcision? An indispensable masquerade/a comedy acted with a specialist's expertise?

Finally women, who of course are actresses. In order to please. But without any qualities of their own. Whence, when speaking of women, the recourse to typographic signs, various kinds of suspension markers, bracketing, quotations marks, parentheses, cuts in the texts, exclamations, and . . . As "Dass sie 'sich geben,' selbst noch, wenn sie—sich geben." "That they '. . .' even when they—'. . . .' "

Women—the deal. For—the game. What is still, and always, hypnotic is when there is still a blank left blank. That can be dealt only by pretending it to be what it is not: still a blank. The game goes on and the blank is given a suit. Or rather is covered up, since it can take on any suit. Woman is so artistic. . . So well disguised, made up, masked. . . The comedy of the other that she plays *so* artistically only because she "is" not in it, has no personal involvement. Remains—the blank?

*In footnote 94 of his translation, Walter Kaufman glosses passage thus: *"Dass sie 'sich geben,' selbst noch, wenn sie—sich geben.* Literally that they 'give themselves' (that is, act, play a part, pose as . . .) even when they—give themselves." The French translation of the German text is here closer to the original since it reproduces Nietzsche's pun on "sich geben," with the distinction between "se donner" and "se donner pour." This expression "se donner pour" is a key term throughout the essay "Veiled Lips," with "pour" repeated over and over again as a one-word reprise of this complex idea.—Tr.

Castrating, of course, is not a simple amputation. Except as it is seen by the same, who categorizes it thus in his theater: as a threat. In order to frighten himself. Castrating is the "absolute" spot in the economy of signs. The absurd: which is not sublated, nor repeated in any way at all. Neither event, nor phenomenon, nor form, nor ideality. . . That which cannot be represented. Not the unrepresentable in the sense of opposite, negative, reverse. For that would once again amount to the same thing. As mirror, blank, hole. That which cannot be represented—in its economy. That which is—not re-presentable in it. Presentable.

Whence all the storytelling to get her to give herself all the same —to put in at least a token appearance. Though it will always be a case of her giving herself out to be. Even though one may well be deceived. Among, between, the veils of the one, of the other, some misunderstanding may still, at times, subsist. As a shot missing its mark. Hitting: some thing.

But, in general, she poses as . . . (se donne pour.) As a result of being nothing in this theater but a nothing that resists representation, and also of being an apparatus that sometimes gets in the way, she interprets the generalization of posing as. . . Because she is castrated, she is the threat of castration. She might act as prompter for the whole scene because she stays outside this way. In the wings. But also outside the scene of the action in a wider sense.

Thus: she is disguised for the performance of representation, hidden in the wings—where she doubles up her own role as other, as well as same—, beyond all that is taking place.

This beyond is nothing that can be called truth, unless so many doublings of parentheses and quotation marks are used that it gets lost in them all. This beyond is none of these/her wrappings, even if she seems still to be there. The/a woman is not to be reabsorbed into truth, or appearances, or semblances. Provided that she still manages to withold herself from the generalization of the stage set. All the more since that set would now like to treat itself/her as woman. Hold her also in the veils of love. Self-love. Signify her in some way herself. Which is impossible.

So therefore she is unable to talk about herself as he does, without getting lost in the process. Illusion spun by the master to seize hold of her again in what she says. But, as master—and in every sense, non-sense, counter-meaning, double meaning . . . —he cannot hear her. Can scarcely find anything to talk back to. Which sets things off again, thanks to a negation or denial. To the nth degree. The operation is always the same.

To talk about her—even supposing a woman could do it—to try and talk about her, comes down to exposing oneself to being only the object, the aim, of a repetition of negation, of denial. To lending oneself to a reexclusion, a repression, outside the general performance of representation. By masters, of all types, who quarrel over the scene. But, however little one gives oneself (se donne)—in order to take back (which cannot and may not be avoided) a formula that has already been produced, by a man talking about women—one always runs the risk, also, of posing as . . . (se donner pour.)

What comes of this pretense? Above all not to want to take control of it. Pretend to be . . . whatever you like. That is, according to your need or your desire. This "posing as" will actually be a bonus. The bonus that, as yet, plays no part in her economy. This "posing as" is not her due. She strays into it, without finding herself.

Unless she is reduced to the master's desire: coin whose value is equal to the credit invested in the wrapping by the work of nature. Her only value is an assumed value. In herself, she has none. Can have none. She can only possess herself, trade herself, as a representative of something else. If she were to be attributed anything as an essential quality, this would amount to forgetting, or wishing to forget, that she plays her part so well only because it is not her due, gives her no advantage. Unless she wants in fact to take part in the master's game. In which she cannot win. . . Indeed, never. Nothing: her "absolute" ruin.

The/a woman never signs up for the game without losing herself. And as she does not know how to play: losing radically. She must give up her gender, or die "in actual fact." Which can happen to her. One might write: it is "her" happening." And not laugh.

But, beyond, she might sub-sist.
In herself she has what it takes to sub-sist.

Statement that makes a spot on the text. Dropping the quotation marks, the parentheses, the dashes . . . the veils, the framework, the distance. . . Which is inconceivable in public. Stripping off a few strata, deposits, of truth/lie, being/appearances, beautiful/ugly, good/evil, simulacrum/"truth". . . A few layers of blanks with different decorations, colors, suits. Since several centuries of silence have taken on quite a number of roles: echo, place, interval, abyss, thing, possibility of repetition, or articulation . . . mirror. . .

That would make a sign of something moving beyond, falling short. Of something out-of place, out-of-context, in everything said, written, painted, played. That always arises from and depends upon a certain specula(riza)tion. Which explains the master's desire in regard to taking possession of that (male) other.

And whether or not woman wants castration, whether or not she believes in that operation, and finds it casting her again as seductress, isn't this/the id still thinking on the male side? This is still what man's woman would be like. And, perhaps, the masculine's feminine? This (male) other over which he hangs a veil to attest to his truth as a man. But from which he will derive what he needs to question the rightness of his judgments past and present. As if drawing from a well of uncertainty that has not been—and doubtless never will be—formulated adequately.

This is what the value of any of man's truths would be like: it stands against a non-background of its form. To make it apparent is always a piece of extreme daring. Shameless effrontery that is worth its weight in gold. Whence the need for wraps of all kinds.

Whereas, on the women's side, it would be possible to manage without gold. She doesn't really need it. Even in the desire for an ornamentation she has no belief in. But which might possibly seduce the other. Though not necessarily. If she plays the game, it is as if with death—the death of man?—insofar as she puts on a show.

For her, gold is not indispensable. Her relation to exchange can do without that pledge. She has a relation to herself that has no need of that guarantee dividing and joining the one (male or female) and the other. In the quest to enjoy the value of her form, being covered, especially by gold, is of no avail. She needs only to embrace herself. Women need only to embrace each other for their truth to have a place—matter and form intertwined in the instant, without abyss or eternity.

Man lacks this operation. Hence the "content" and the representation of his truth. Alone or with other men he cannot "embrace himself": he cannot exchange himself with the other while remaining in the same. And should the other serve as a sheath for him, at best he will make a wrapping of it, but not an embracing. He who wraps keeps matter in one form but makes no exchange as he remains in the same "truth."

Is it not because woman can do this that her operation as castratrix has been invented? But this is to think of her solely as they do in the men's camp. And thereby deprive her of a relation to her "own" sex. Of any auto-affection that has not been determined by and for the masculine. Which woman could manage without. Though this is not to say that she must manage without. She may manage without in the relation with herself.

She does not set herself up as *one*, as a (single) female unit. She is not closed up or around one single truth or essence. The essence of a truth remains foreign to her. She neither has nor is a being. And she does not oppose a feminine truth to the masculine truth. Because this would once again amount to playing the—man's—game of castration. If the female sex takes place by embracing itself, by endlessly sharing and exchanging its lips, its edges, its borders, and their "content," as it ceaselessly becomes other, no stability of essence is proper to her. She has a place in the openness of a relation to the other whom she does not take into herself, like a whore, but to whom she continuously gives birth.

And she has no need *once* to be a mother, *one* day to produce *one* child, to make her sex the place of unceasing birthing. To be woman, she does not have to be mother, unless she wants to set a limit to her growth and her gift for life. Motherhood is only one specific way to fulfill the operation: giving birth. Which is never one, unique, and definitive. Except from the male standpoint.

The/a woman can sub-sist by already being double in her self: both the one and the other. Not: one plus an other, more than one. More than. She is "foreign" to the unit. And to the countable, to quantification. Therefore to the more than, as it relates to something already quantifiable, even were it a case of disrupting the operations. If it were necessary to count her/them in units—which is impossible—each unit would already be more than doubly (her). But that would have to be understood in another way. The (female) one being the other, without ever being either one or the other. Ceaselessly in the exchange between the one and the other. With the result that she is always already othered but with no possible identification of her, or of the other. Who is not even a foundation for identification: some mirror, for examples. There will therefore never be a her and her other. The possessive, the mark of belonging, does not belong to her. Nor does the reflexive. That comes back/down to the same thing. Re-produces some sign in order to take possession of it/oneself.

The/a woman does not simply make (herself) signs. That existing mediation remains im-proper to her. She cannot relate it to herself. And even if that manifestation should correspond to her, there would be no need to see it as a necessary phenomenon. The feminine goes beyond "phenomenology." Were it not for the demands of the echonomy of sameness. Because "she" affects herself already (within herself) without the appearance of a sensible sign. She has no overriding need to produce herself under any form whatever. At least as far as (she is) herself. She gives herself out to be—herself if one falls for it—because she herself is unable to present herself. But this lack is also the source of her "bonus." If her "logic" did not shy away from pluses or minuses.

In herself: does not mean in the intimacy of a "soul" or a "spirit." As it risks being understood at a first approximation. Provisionally, let us drop what this "approximation" may imply in the way of detour, straying, repressing, sublimation . . . of the depth of woman. She falls back into a depth of thought: that goes right to the bottom of things, beyond appearances, would therefore be difficult to penetrate because it is more internal, more secret, but also more durable because it is not subject to the fluctuations of the sensations, of the perceptible world. From time to time it is worthwhile to flatten out this "inside" (of the spirit), bring it to the surface. Though it has never ceased being a surface. A protection-projection screen that, by dint of returning upon the self to the point of doubling up and circling the self, is nonetheless superficial in its full extent. Planes that elude, exclude, keep on the outside, external to her, and limit with their developments the depth of the other.

Reserve: the abyss. To go back to it. Except for him—and even then . . . providing he does not fall—depth is essentially superficial. To give depth back as what she is would therefore amount to raising the mortgage on it: preventing her from producing any pretense of being: what is.

This plastering over of the depths of truth, in order to play with them on the basis of a display that will not be exhausted too quickly, also reduces in its game the truth of the other. Let it appear: risk.

Putting it aside in the generalization of the simulacrum is a way of keeping something in reserve. Borrowing from the reserves of the other, that has perhaps been a not-giving-oneself-out-to-be-the-same: which it is not.

Into *her* depth, the scene might still collapse. Not into the abyss of meaning, its inversion or aversion. Let's leave the abyss, the chasm, . . . Here "simply" in that deep female other that sub-sists. Beneath the general echonomy of truth—therefore also of appearance, simulacrum, suspense between, even of that reserve: the undecidable—woman is still deep. The fact that she may have served, may still serve, as mirror of every kind does not solve this remainder: extra, deep. Which upsets the whole thing.

This depth is, in fact, neither single, nor essential, nor a potential for foundation and its excess—the abyss—nor the hole-scaffolding of the scene's systematization which cannot be rigorously deduced or derived therefrom. The fact that she has been travestied in this manner amounted to putting everything to work so as to set her up as an outside. The other outside.

Now the/a woman is not one. And this way of reducing the outside marks the limit of the method of questioning. Not identical to self, the/a woman does not answer *one* question. The question that would be appropriate to her is always and forever impossible to formulate even if one wanted to make the effort.

Short of giving up all principles? But that would still be staking in one's game that against which they fixed the rights of the same. It's better to keep principles so as to glimpse what another gender might not be about. Whose depth cannot be represented except in the form of error and appearance. With this error still being a property of being. A representation of the other as perpetual becoming and change—wanderings. At best, errancy. Because she has no place in the time of essence, of durability, of self-identity, the other errs: reverse of the sames.

To compose oneself an object to suit one's fantasy and believe henceforth that one would possess it wholly as the lover does with his beloved, the father with the child: what joy than in possessing! —but here it is the appearance that suffices us. We imagine the objects *that we can attain* in such a way that their possession seems most valuable to us: we compose to suit our pride the enemy that we *hope* to conquer; and in the same way the woman and the child. (*Joyful Wisdom*, posthumous fragment 11:34)*

In the clearing of a blind spot of truth, a space is opened up for the games of the imagination in the possession of a property—in this way we can have it with more subtlety.

Something that no longer has any secret place to hide in could not escape us, since the full knowledge of the thing is appropriation enough. But if there is no secret, where can there be reserve? How is the will-to-have, the will-to-keep, to be perpetuated?

Full awareness—dissimulation that hides (itself). The most subtle kind of possession.

The depth of woman cannot be closed up over having—knowledge of a secret. Except from the point of view of the truth in which she is played as a store (of) dissimulation: her representation therein will never have been anything but pretense, in a different way. She is denigrated or valued according to the historical moment. And—both at the same time.

The thing that the depth of woman is supposed to be the hiding place and hiding mechanism for is what representation obliterates even from the visible. For "she," also, is visible. But she is not repeated, reproduced, in traditional representation because she is already split "within herself." And the echonomy in being cannot account for this. For fear of putting all its properties into question: one, simple, self-identical, grounded, derivable, etc. Even if that economy goes so far as to admit the work of repetition in presence, the splitting of the unit within itself remains foreign to it.

Therefore the *access* to woman's depth. Since neither the female one nor the other is separable as such in the appearance or in the abyss, and hidden from view only within the simulacrum. With each female one already upset and overwhelmed, she neither is nor becomes the other. And to say that she signifies wandering, errancy, comes down to mixing these up in the other—of the same. A moving stake in the articulation of essential definitions or values, secret resource for phenomena, necessity for the dissimulation that is affirmed in the game.

*Le Gai Savoir: Fragments inedits 1881–1882*, texte et variantes etablis par G. Colli et M. Montinari (Paris: Gallimard, 1967), p. 310.—Tr.

89

It seems then that she plays the game, without playing it. In fact she has no equipment available to play with. But her functioning "within herself" is ludic: the single aim of her physical or mental activity would be the pleasure it procures. But with no consciousness.

Therefore she doesn't strictly speaking play. A game, if it implies risk, cannot be separated from the desire to win, or lose, or accumulate: more or less. Luck is still the chance that assists or even substitutes for capitalization. And if expense is possible, pleasure does not come free. By way of proof: it is a factor of the value assigned to the pawns, their hierarchy, their falling by mastery or by chance—or is it the mastery of chance?—to one player or the other at the end of the game.

Is exchange, once free of the laws of truth, in fact more cynically capitalist? Liberalism without restraint because freed of customs duties by chance? "Morally not deliberate," therefore without error. Luck—the deal. Can only be dealt out for what he/she is not. Is never simply dealt as such (male or female) for fear of no longer believing it. The strength of this dissimulation reverts to the master-player. What does he lose? There no longer falls to his lot: pleasure.

The stake of woman's ludism has no fixed value. Value is never attributed. Even though her having no value may be the cause of her despisal does not spoil, for her, the pleasure of endlessly exchanging herself "within herself"; does not cut off her access to depth. That throws off the opposition deliberate/lucky. Except insofar as it applies to the chance of her gender: female. Once this casting has been made—and it also goes beyond, and stops short of, truth, appearances, semblances—pleasure comes to her with no forethought. Unless she gives up that excess of good fortune: being born a woman. The whole game is set up so that she should do so. But "within herself" she never signs up. She doesn't have the equipment.

As, to take "an example," the division subject-predicate, subject-object.

So, when she touches herself (again), who is "she"? And "herself"? Inseparable, "she" and "herself" are part the one of the other, endlessly. They cannot really be distinguished, though they are not for all that the female same, nor the male same. That can be reassembled within some whole. This is to say again, or further, that it would be impossible to decide definitively which "of the two" would be "she" and which "herself."

Thus—by a (perhaps misleading?) comparison with discourse—the identity of the subject can no longer be established through its relation to the object, and none of these functions is more important than the other. With this disjunction signifying their yielding to discursivity itself. And even if "to touch oneself," for the masculine gender, is defined as that which begins to set up the distinction subject-predicate, subject-object, in the most archaic fashion, i.e., in the relation of attribution: x is (to, in, . . . ) y—which still allows passivity to have a place in auto-affection, or else a suspension between activity and passivity in the attribution of being—it will never be known who/what is x, who/what is y in the female. Each female is at the same time "x" and "y" but not by being addition, subtraction, division. . . Not even multiplication, as this would risk closing up the volume. With difficulty, it is true. . . Since each side cannot be dissociated from the other without thereby forming with it an angle of which the span would be a or b. . .

The values are indeed impossible to calculate, determine, as-sign, . . . Therefore *are* not. Perhaps woman is predicated in the ab-solute. This operation then derives from the masculine gender. This is the case with female objects, that are variously qualified accord-ing to their utility. Predicatable insofar as she is an "object in gen-eral," the/a woman remains external to the objective. From this outside position she grounds its economy—by being castrated, she threatens castration. Glimpsing that she may sub-tend the logic of predication without its functioning having anything properly to do with her, leads to the fear that she may intervene and upset every-thing: the death of the subject would be nothing less. A ground rises up, a montage of shapes disintegrates. The horror of the abyss, attributed to woman. Loss of identity—death.

Her life is not something else: death. Death is always minus one, less simple than one imagines. It resists belonging, it sub-sists be-yond appropriation. It is still left over. There is always *more of* death, than the one already identified. And the/a woman who withholds herself from the identifiable, therefore threatens—with death. A residue left over by the set up of representation: she lives in death.

She does not die from it. Except as a subject. This life in death sustains the death that is the life of the spirit, a death that gives (back) life by dint of the fact that the other (male or female), who buttresses it, is not really dead. Only as subject; that which the subject of discourse uses for nourishment. Should his wish for nourishment find another end, this subject becomes bloodless.

She nourishes. Or yet: she suffers, ails, enjoys, she even threatens. She—affected by a predicate without an object. She—object of predication. The almost inverted project of predication: an absolute subject subjected to predication in the absolute. And, by all appearances, immediately so. Whereas the subject—a subject—defers his reassembly into a totality through the enumeration and articulation of his properties. She grounds predication without strictly speaking being marked by it: she is not determined through the application of such or such a quality. She sub-sists "within herself" beneath discourse. As that which has also been called prime matter.

Out of the storehouse of matter all forms are born. She brings them into the world, she "produces." From between her lips comes every new figure: a warm glowing heat comes out of that self-embrace and becomes "visible." But once, one single time and one instant only: beauty. Afterward, or by default and repetition, there are veils. Unless there be a divine reality.

For seeing the ultimate beauties in a work, no knowledge or good will is sufficient; this requires the rarest of lucky accidents: The clouds that veil these peaks have to lift for once so that we see them glowing in the sun. Not only do we have to stand in precisely the right place in order to see this, but the unveiling must have been accomplished by our own soul because it needed some external expression and parable, as if it were a matter of having something to hold on to and retain control of itself. But it is so rare for all of this to coincide that I am inclined to believe that the highest peaks of everything good, whether it be a work, a deed, humanity, or nature, have so far remained concealed and veiled from the great majority and even from the best human brings. But what does unveil itself for us, *unveils itself for us only once.* The Greeks, to be sure, prayed: "Everything beautiful twice and and even three times!" They implored the gods with good reason, for ungodly reality gives us the beautiful either not at all, or once only. I mean to say that the world is overfull of beautiful things, but nevertheless poor, very poor when it comes to beautiful moments, and unveilings of these things. But perhaps this is the most powerful magic of life: it is covered by a veil interwoven with gold, a veil of beautiful possibilities, sparkling with promise, resistance, bashfulness, mockery, pity, and seduction. Yes, life is a woman! (*The Gay Science*, p. 339).

The possible that is reserved, the modesty that is bashful, the seduction that is elusive and promises—resistingly, mockingly, pityingly—to give itself: life as a woman.

The return of what is repressed, while she is kept in repression. Beneath a veil interwoven with gold. She thus gives herself only when covered over with a wrapping of values already elsewhere and defined otherwise than she herself/values themselves. Beauty: the birth of the form is lost therein. This (self-)embrace will no longer take place. Except in certain myths of origin: God is thought to create man by shaping him between his hands. Act already, already will? Its repetition in art?

For her, it would need "the rarest of lucky accidents." For her? Or for a "soul" to notice her, once the unveiling has been accomplished "by our own soul, because it needed some external expression and parable, as if it were a matter of having something to hold on to and retain control of itself."

The soul—woman curled up in an interiorness that is affected only by the mediation of forms, and in order to become master of itself in the appropriation of a production. The femaleness of the soul? The pleasure of woman declines even if some—rarest—coincidence sometimes reminds us—o revelation!—of her "generic" relation to beauty. But, in that case, only *once!* The Greeks doubtless used to pray: "Twice and thrice, everything beautiful." —Alas! they had good reason to call on the gods...

For it is precisely repetition that prevents her from returning. Repetition embroiders the gold veil that covers beauty. Perhaps indeed this is the greatest charm of life... Which is as much as to say that suspense has more attractions than pleasure. That it has become pleasure: the expectation, desirable in mastery, of gods who will not return again.

The break between gods and men: the interdict-impossibility of Dionysiac sensuality, the virtual renunciation of Apollo's enchantment unless it be to privilege identification's value as mask, while at the same time forgetting what the gods were already obscuring, isn't this what claims universalization under the law of castration? Identity is marked through the property of the name, a morphological economy that already leaves back in an earlier past the burgeoning individuation of a single form-figure: that is apparent, and still tangible. She is beautiful and also has that fragility that comes to her as a result of no longer touching everything: from being distinguished as such in the moment when she first makes her appearance. But dead from (this) birth?

Death relayed by a whole chain of logical combinations/the mortality of woman arising from her separation from the "earth" that sustained her growth. She rises up erect, in full view, alone, detached and threatened with death by being thus cut off from her "roots."

Sub-sists the death-life that does not reach, or renounces? individuation in order to keep hold of the self-embrace, nearness, simultaneity, . . . She remains, close, but foreign to mastery, to any form of sublation into the ever threatening representation. Buried in the deepest "depths," primitively, in the swamps of oblivion.

Later the rise of fair appearance is repressed—but only for a moment—when she detaches herself from every whole. Afterward: she is taken back into forms that are abstract, eternal because they have had no beginning, that are neither beautiful nor ugly, but true (well born), and whose justification is to avoid pain and pleasure, the violence of the senses, expenditure, a nearness without distinction, . . . blood. Refusal, negatives, that inaugurate the ethico-political order of patriarchy?

☆

A woman—the other—will be asked to set the seal of necessity upon this/her burial. A woman, in truth: of divine reality. A divinity conceived in the head of the God of gods. Well born—without a mother.

The female ideal—the femininity of woman serving as mediation between the viscera of the earth and the most heavenly god: the father of the gods. Whose daughter she is said to be, since she came into the light of day having never known the darkness of a mother's womb.

Woman engendered by the father alone—operation whereby values are overtuned, reversed, in the thought of the man-father. Hidden here is the secret of the production of the idea—woman. Conception of a wholly spiritual nature, that represses and denies/negates a conception that still remembers blood. Femininity will put up the security. Ensuring, while also being a possible mediation, that the relations between woman-mother and man-father are cut.

Femininity—that part of his thought God splits off in order to assist him in the totality of his work. ("With regard to what I intend to do during the next ten years, I have need of women." (Letter from Nietzsche to P. Gast, March 4, 1882.) Staying between: the gods on high, men, and the gods below. Organizing the place of each of them, arbitrating quarrels, supervising the wars between those driven by a violent love of fame. . . She is conciliatory, benevolent. . . Seducing everyone and everything to accept the peace afforded by "justice": a thought that stays in the middle. Neither anarchist nor despot. Interval of neutrality. At least in appearance. Because "I am unreservedly for male in everything/save marrying one—/enthusiastically on my father's side" (Aeschylus, *The Eumenides*, ll. 737–738).*

Femininity—the father's indispensable intermediary in putting his law into force. The simulacrum that makes the false pass into the true, obscures the difference between, substitutes for it a spacing of pretense: the neutrality of femininity. Which even God needed in order to pass for, to give himself out to be the only creator. To make himself out to be—what he is not. Which will be attributed to woman. And she need only forget that she owes life also to her mother for that loan to become her most divine reality. Life as femininity—the opposite. Everything is made to lead up to it. And she will play it/herself all the better by not being there.

Femininity—the secret of production of the sophism. Of the oracle's "lie," of the double dissimulation in the word of a god: with Apollo declaring that the mother plays no part in generation. His proof: the spiritual daughter of Olympian Zeus, more perfect offspring than those any goddess every gave birth to (*idem*, ll. 658–666).

A phantasy of the father of the gods, lent to the God, will henceforward decide the right of everyone. And, as even the divinest woman doesn't understand much about the discourse of truth, she repeats the lines perfectly: "No mother ever gave me birth: I am unreservedly for male in everything, etc." (*Idem*, pp. 736–738). Save marrying one.

"In the father's camp" there is no more sexual intercourse. Woman remains "foreign," "merely cultivates the shoot/host for a guest—if

---

*Translation by Paul Roche, New American Library paperback edition.—Tr.

no god blights" (*idem*, ll. 658–659). Man, product of the male seed alone. "But I and my mother *are* one blood presumably" questions Apollo (*idem*, l. 606). Woman also. This genetic mistake draws the whole scene of truth into a semblance: the reign of femininity. Reasonable, even speculative, a little warlike: armed to the teeth, but a mediator nonetheless. Between the high and the low, and all the extremes, but with the direction always being projected from the same point. To make a circle, perhaps.

Femininity is part and parcel of the patriarchal order. Woman is hidden in the thought of the father. When she gives birth to herself fully equipped—even with weapons. She is veiled, her beauty hidden. Only the shape appears anymore. Therefore, not the woman. She would no longer touch herself. Only the face sees/is seen. And the voice clearly expresses the father's wishes, which she translates into words all men—all citizens—can hear. Femininity knows about seductiveness, knows how to attract and snare in the folds of her garments—a dissimulation that is multiplied, that multiplies her. She calculates her effects, her blows. . .

But the incantation that moves, troubles, sings—of the impossibility of clearly saying anything, that says everything, every woman, all together, the female one and the other with no differentiation or distinction that can be put into words, this "style" of evocation, *harmony*, is missing in her. Daughter of the father alone, she repeats his discourse without understanding much, fulfills his law by enacting it everywhere, in the midst of everything, mediating for everyone, ready to use guile and charm to do the work of violence. At least according to appearances. Gives herself out to be. . .

A murder has occurred—femininity appeases the anger, calls for the blood to be forgotten, lulls vengeance to sleep with sweet words, promises homage, honor, festivals, rites, sacrifices, a religious silence, if only the "old children—no children—of Night" will agree to retire into a "primal crypt of the earth" and remain "bland and benign to our land" (*idem*, ll. 1034–1040).

Femininity doubles the burial of the mother when she buries the chorus. So that Zeus may triumph, "the god of forensic" (*idem*, l. 974).

She needed all her powers of persuasion to conquer the savage behavior of a nature that still resists the logic of truth. The snarlings, shrieks, grumbles, howls, the hurtful reproaches—addressed to the gods, no less—the thirst for blood. . . The oaths, squabbles, exclamations, questionings, . . . the laments, the groans, the curses, . . . the songs, the hymns, the delirious noise, . . . All at once, all the women at once, with no one identified. . . And the dances, the races, the leaps, . . . the movement. . . All at once and together. Until the final silence. The chorus mastered, repressed into a subterranean crypt.

The law of the father needed femininity—a replica of a woman—in order to take the upper hand over the mother's passion, as well as the woman's pleasure.

Then will come all kinds of music, no longer the chorus. That is taken over as soon as it is reborn. Organized in a quite different way. The whole thing together is calculated, summated, composed, attuned, with the "actors" and the "instruments" the chorus lacks. Which could not be rehearsed/repeated. Its beauty could occur only once. If repetition should have a place *within* the chorus, it means something quite other: the impossibility of unity. Thus the same thing is sung therein, a second time. But "the other" is not separated from the same: does not represent it, figure it, reproduce it. The (female) one and the other "say" the same, together. Without the female one or without the other—which would be the same, inseparable, impossible to identify in their exchange, and yet at least two —this harmony no longer takes place.

In harmony, the id touches itself again, and that embrace, which corresponds well to a state of nature, would let the gaze wander further than is possible when something visible that cannot be discriminated from natural contiguity had already, it seems, been excluded from its field of vision. Because they have "overcome" that kind of visibility, the forms will no doubt be clearer, more elegant, more "pure," but they will already be perverted in the appearance of "lying" shows. Which are comforting in their beauty, seductive, appeasing. But carry us farther and farther away from the Dionysiac re-source.

One turn more, and Socratism is set up. Despising appearance for its mere beauty. Socrates will yet use its forms and fill them with meaning. He places art in the service of truth, which amounts to saying that he takes hold of it as such and gives it another teleology than the perceptible one it had. He claims to curb those corrupting veils into the "proper" sense, failing to realize that those very wrappings take the place of vehicles (of truth) for him. The forms-ideas are borrowed from Apollo, but his beauty, though certainly still useful for teaching purposes, is from now on subject to the Good.

Something of the Dionysiac has in fact been held over, if nowhere else in the *pathos* of death: the supreme good. Socrates desiring death, and achieving it thanks to a drink given him by the citizens, signifies his allegiance to the Dionysiac. It is by this means that he will take away its power. Those wrenching contradictions that he bore within himself are resolved by his death that pays off the debt knowledge owes to the primitive-mother-nature. The life of Socrates is still a tragedy. But this first and last hero of theory would leave to his posterity only the symbolic repetition of (his) death: the death "for a laugh" of the philosopher whose potion is the *logos*.

No longer to be able to die is also no longer to be able to live: to be cut off from the tragic. To be installed in definitive forms, that no longer know any roots in the natural world, in which it is no longer possible to see how much of nature they mask: the teleological ex-stasis serves as a double that entraps—but the trap of the trap operates as a negation—something of the becoming of birth that has been lost. And if Apollo is this beautiful only so that he can make us forget the horror still revealed by Dionysos, the contemplation of the supreme Good is now a duty, not so much by being an overt consolation, an assistance necessary to soften the terror of life, but because the true imposes itself as the principle governing the will to live the good life. Once all the passions are ordained by that unique cause, the passionate excesses or surpluses to living according to truth will be resolved in the divine possession.

Whether possessed or not, what did Socrates amputate from ecstasy? Or what did he add?

Did he take away its illusion? No, but he modified its economy. The veil of appearance is masked and stolen from the immediate pleasure-desire of the beautiful. It is *used* in the reproduction of truth. And one would need to go back over all the mimes-copies to demonstrate—if there were still anyone available to watch the show —all the illusion apparent in the philosopher's transport in God. Deferred up to the point of that final ex-altation, illusion would reveal itself in its "pure" state, but in a jouissance that would escape in the very moment it befalls the will, and the pleasure, of the person who enjoys. In fact, this ec-stasy would be mortal. People would not recover from it. And people would not agree to anyone else recovering from it, but would kill him all over again.

Illusion no longer has the freedom of the city. It is no longer the companion, the adornment of life. It fascinates like something beyond good living that must be expelled, wiped out of everyday life. That illusion, in the final analysis, determines the laws of society cannot and must not be seen. The fair appearance that now assuages the presentiment of a tragic end: death, is suspect and despicable because it is a link to a life, and its only worth lies in its return to eternity. And in the view of eternity, death is no more than an almost comic repetition.

Appearance has been split off from the will: it is not worthy of an application of the will. Quite to the contrary, it must be separated from the will. So that it can be invested in the belief in a Good that can be imitated unreservedly because it was not merely likely, a recourse to the painful destiny of man, but that meaning of life which, once found, entails a serenity that cannot be attained in its constancy. Apollo's dream of splendor, inciting to action by temporarily anesthetizing suffering, would henceforward be a secondary pleasure, reserved for artists who are dangerous if it/they distract from the search for truth.

Now that god was still heralded as, among other things, the god of illusion, and of the need to dream if one is to live. He spoke of the divine character of the will, and again of the eyes closed to the absurdity of life, if one is to continue to live and act despite the monstrousness, the deformity, the atrocity to be seen everywhere. Socrates does not admit that the natural gaze should thus be abandoned with enthusiasm. And yet he leads up to the same notion while at the same time taking from it the joy of joyously accepted blindness. The reality, the objectivity, of forms still, imperceptibly, has a part in the dream. No mortal eye can open upon an idea. It will therefore be fitting to see only with the soul. Philosophy teaches the eyelids to close tighter and tighter to bar anything still presented by the senses, teaches the gaze to turn inward to the soul, that screen for the projection of ideal images. The horror of nature is magicked away: it will be seen only though the blind of intelligible categories, and the weaknesses that ultimately will lay man low will be laid at the door of an insufficiently lofty point of view.

Socrates dreams, no doubt about it. But he doesn't know he does, doesn't want to know. He dreams of no longer dreaming: he can no longer see that he can no longer see (nature). This double negative is the basis for the philosophical order as such. Forgetting—as in a dream—that one forgets as a result of forgetting—willed as a dream —has become an abyss, it is blocked off from the desire to unveil truth. Desire henceforward subject to the law, prescribed by morality, and in which the infatuations and pains of the will will be tempered-suspended in a duly organized hierarchy of progress, with no useless orgies or expenditures.

The will, of course, does not will the truth. Truth kills will by her will to live well. And Socrates, who still wills, will die because of it. However wise he may be, he in fact expected no more than to pass beyond: the truth. But later on. And at the moment? He was cruelly optimistic. The citizens' judgment, in a mime-drama played out in public, proves this. But the surface legality of the scenario neutralizes its barbarousness. Everything goes off very peacefully—apart from the shrieks of a few women who are hurriedly whisked away— and no blood is shed. Death is imperceptible. It is merely noted, as a matter of objective, verifiable fact, that the whole body stiffens and goes cold.

What else could be the death of the theoretician? Just a suppression of the pain of living. Whose excesses little befit a city organized beneath the scepter of the father of the gods.

☆

It is Apollo, the farsighted one who is always already speaking, who first commanded the murder of the mother. Thus wiping away, denying, the illegitimacy of his own birth? Blood shed to confirm that he belongs to the law of the father alone.

Necessary sacrifice to order in the home. Apollo—the brother, in God, of Athena. Patriarchal right/blood ties. Orestes who slits his mother's throat takes refuge in the temple of the god who is subject to the wishes of Zeus alone. The women who cry out for revenge are thrown out of the temple as if they were bringing in filth.

Apollo no longer hears the chorus. He drives the "rabble" of women away from his oracle.

Out I say from here. / Leave this edifice at once. / Get off and gone from my prophetic holy place, / or feel the strike of a winged and coruscating snake/ whipped from my golden bow, / to make you froth away your life in spasms/ of black and man-drawn bile—/ spewing out your clotted human suckings. / This is not fitting residence for you to board. / Yours is a place of sentences:/ where heads are chopped, eyes gouged, throats cut,/ and seed is crushed from striplings spoiled in flower. / Yes, a place of mutilations, stonings—/ helpless wailings long drawn out/ from men pinned through the spine. / Do you want to know what turns the stomach of the Gods?/ Those feasts you find so charming. / Your whole shape and mien give you away. / Freaks like you should make your hole/ deep in some blood-beslobbered lion's den/ and not come rubbing off your filth/ on those beside these sacred mantic spots. / Get gone, you goatish rabble with no goatherd:/ No god's love is lost on such a flock. (*Eumenides*, ll. 179–197)

The wisdom of Apollo—his cruelty. The serenity of unions blessed by the gods, the sweetest joys of mortals, the couch where fate weds man and woman—their cruelties. The father devouring his children, the husband going off to a war among men—at stake: another woman, the virgin daughter sacrificed in order to win victory, the husband's infidelity, his return, accompanied by yet another woman—the anger of the wife, the mother.

The god's deafness to the Erinnye. The voices of the divine women of the earth reduced to silence by the goddess of the heights: the daughter of the Father. The chorus of women/ Athena. The mother/ Athena. The daughter/ Athena. The woman/ Athena. All the women, all together—I-we, thou-you—wounded, humiliated, bloody, suppliant, breathless, exhausted from their pursuit—without wings—of the murderer who has the means to fly and get over the seas, with technique. The women—thou or you, I or we—weary, sleepy, in a dream . . . freezing, shivering with pain beneath the whip of a ferocious tormentor.

The justice that is mindful of blood/the justice of the immortal one; a semblance, but cruel. The blood shed on the ground disappears forever. The earth sops up the traces of the crime. Forgetfulness.

There remains—Hades, to whom mortals must give an account, under the earth, Hades who sees everything and inscribes it in his memory. On the opposite side, the law of the gods on high. Their truth, their beauty, their immortality. In between—Athena: horror concealed, wound masked, the difference in values covered over. Pretense of the God of gods—standing in the long white robe that veils even her feet.

Deception, in the service of the master. Treachery, to the father's advantage. Chaining women to household drudgery, but, for herself, preferring public life. Favoring boys, but refusing marriage, her father's virgin. She who inspires and protects institutions. Without any doubt, virile, if she lets fall her tunic. Armed: femininity. Playing with every disguise. Childish, if need be, without ever having known childhood: brotherly, all the better to betray confidence; simulating a friendship for women, while persuading them to go away and not give any trouble, down into caves and underground lairs, private homes. Leading astray, making mad, inciting men to break their oaths, to murder, to die—without ever shedding her divine candor.

The ambivalence the god feels for the mother, the woman, is incarnate in the character of the goddess. What will henceforth be called women's deceitfulness. Which is merely a projection of the Father. Adorned, femininity—the father's thought appearing over female authority. By taking over maternal power, by swallowing it, introjecting it, he engenders, produces, this daughter who (only) gives herself out to be what she is not: a simulacrum borrowed by the God to help him in his work, establish his empire. A semblance that claims to do without body, death. Seduction rules in appearance-*truth*. Also needs beauty, but as a decoy. That touches, therefore, only to achieve some—virile—objective. That no longer affects, is no longer affected by, anything "within herself." Always already standardized according to the father's desire alone. Knowing nothing but the master's jouissance.

What recourse has the son who slaughtered his mother? To cling to the stone effigy of an immortal goddess, kneel, and take in his arms the "statue" of Athena (*Eumenides*, ll. 258–259). Asking for her grace, proving to her his new innocence: he has sacrificed a purificatory pig (the mother/the pig) and the men whom he has approached have suffered no harm (*idem*, ll. 282–285). Therefore he is pure, a good citizen. Fit for life in common with free men. Perhaps even a potential king.

The light of day banishes the crimes of night. Whoever argues judiciously thereby gives evidence of his innocence. A wise man's reason wipes the spots of murder from his hands. Zeus does not consider the flock of women dripping with blood to be worthy of an audience. Athena demands a clear explanation.

The tragedy of women will no longer be heeded. The all of them together, the all of it together, at the same time, and yet with no unity. The (male or female) one and the other, they who are not reduced to the same, and not subordinate to one single one (male or female), will no longer have a place. Songs, hymns, shouts, growling, grumbling, yelping . . . praise and blame . . . delirium and wisdom . . . exclamations, affirmations, interrogations . . . groans, laments, gaiety . . . and dancing, running, leaping. . . All those (male and female) things at once and together. Banished from the order of the city, buried far from the sun, sunk beneath the city, slumbering under the appearance of serenity, calm, peace.

The chorus, cut down, enslaved, humbly yielding to "Persuasion": the femininity of the daughter of Zeus. Who repeats what she is prompted, in a single voice: "Farewell and farewell, with largess for your lot!/ Farewell you men of this city:/ seated by Zeus,/ Loved by the virgin beloved/ Learning discernment at last/ Under the wings of Athena/ And great in the eyes of her father" (*idem*, ll. 1014–1020). The chorus, charmed, tamed, agrees to be enclosed in a crypt, walks toward its tomb, in a religious silence. The antique rites and sacrifices in their cave will honor those goddesses greedy for homage. "Pour out a fellowship in perpetuity/ Made with these guests and these people of Pallas/ Which Zeus the All-seeing, with Fate, has confirmed" (*idem*, ll. 1044–1045).

Pallas—the white veil over her body, the affected candor, the shroud over the woman, the mortal trappings. The pacifying spell of the god of speech.

Do I still have ears? Am I all ears and nothing else? Here I stand in the flaming surf whose white tongues are licking at my feet; from all sides I hear howling, threats, screaming, roaring coming at me, while the old earth-shaker sings his aria in the lowest depths, deep as a bellowing bull, while pounding such an earth-shaking beat that the hearts of even these weather-beaten rocky monsters are trembling in their bodies. Then, suddenly, as if born out of nothing, there appears before the gate of this hellish labyrinth, only a few fathoms away—a large sailboat, gliding along silently as a ghost. Oh, what ghostly beauty! How magically it touches me! Has all the calm and taciturnity of the world embarked on it? Does my happiness itself sit in this quiet place—my happier ego, my second, departed self? Not to be dead and yet no longer alive. A spiritlike intermediate being: quietly observing, gliding, floating. As the boat that with its white sails moves like an immense butterfly over the dark sea. Yes! To move *over* existence! That's it! That would be something! It seems as if the noise here has led me into fantasies. All great noise leads us to move happiness into some quiet distance. When a man stands in the midst of his own noise, in the midst of his own surf of plans and projects, then he is apt also to see quiet, magical beings gliding past him and to long for their happiness and seclusion: *women*. He almost thinks that his better self dwells there among the women, and that in these quiet regions even the loudest surf turns into deathly quiet, and life itself into a dream about life. Yet! Yet! Noble enthusiast, even on the most beautiful sailboat there is a lot of noise, and unfortunately much small and petty noise. The magic and the most powerful effect of women is, in philosophical language, action at a distance, *actio in distans;* but this requires first of all and above all,—*distance! (The Gay Science,* p. 60)

From the measure beaten out by the old earth-shaker rises, as if from nothingness, and at a distance, a great sailing-ship that passes silently, gliding like a ghost.

This distant enchanting calm, whose happiness and retirement he longs for, is, it seems, associated with women. The violence of his rhythm would be calmed in the company of these dream creatures in a place where his better self might dwell—like a secret of death, and life that had become its own dream. Creation blossoming out from his throbbing pulse and as if produced by its tumult.

Women would thus float off into death. Always at a distance. Out of reach but well in sight. Allowing the rhythm to pick up without missing a beat. From one hammering to the next, they remain there, calmly. Giving and taking back the dream of their supple spread of canvas.

At a distance, then. And since, left "to themselves," within "themselves," women always come close, it is—always—necessary to push them away. Rape. Rob. Robe.

The distancing of women, their absence—from "themselves" as well—is precisely their "most powerful effect"! Not to be (there), except as—dissimulation of nature. Which is lent them as an operation, bearing the threat of death, whereas they lend themselves to it, almost "by nature."

By nature, (a) woman would seem to be at least double. Her "operation" would be to double. But, naturally, the him/her that is nearest. The him/her that is so near that the figure, the shape, even when visible, are blurred in the immediacy of this "act." With no discrimination of model or reproduction. With no interval that can be framed between the one and the other. Indefinite growth, ironic proliferation of the natural, that it was perhaps necessary to limit for fear it would ruin mastery. As it sank beneath an ever more.

From that ceaseless to-ing and fro-ing that upsets any opposition between here and there, from that endless embrace, from that "in the self" and at the same time and same place in the other, and neither the one nor the other, neither the same and its other, how is an idea to be had? And such an operation remains so foreign to him that, believing he must crack this thing open, that he can only take possession of it through violence, by forcing her/it beyond the present appearances, "man" arms himself with some pointed object—probe, stiletto, sometimes a pen—so he can get inside her/it. Pressing with all his strength to force her out of her retreat. Whereas she always remains open.

But, once he has driven a wedge into her like this, split her into two, he doesn't know how to bring these/her edges back together again. How is the gap thus created to be overcome, how is he to pass over what runs between. Whereas she springs inexhaustibly from the touching together (of her lips), he must now leap from one bank to another.

Attributing its own project to him, the abyss rises (l'abîme ou l'abyme). Because of him bringing his own project to bear, the abyss arises. The break between, the hardening of the edges, the forgotten river that now divides them.

The distance does not come from her, even if, for him, it is at a distance that her seductive charm works. Even if, in the present, he lends her that element of authority. Because he does not wish to see the effect of his operation: the abyss enters. Which holds him off and fascinates him like the attraction of a knife thrust into the other. The other's belly. The other that he no longer approaches simply, except at the risk of his life: some horrendous retaliation for his own act. The removal of one's own self, the decisive incision between the lips that leaves (the other) mute and alluring like the tomb.

From the space thus torn into the fabric, nothing will come but ghosts and simulacra. Dreams of life and death. Placatory veils to mask the destruction that sets up the distant as such.

He has lost nothing thereby but his consciousness. And if, for him, consciousness endlessly swallows everything up, this is because, if it had a bottom to it, he would read there the mark of his crime. Far better to forget it. The bottom of his being would be like this, a nihilation upon which he would erect himself. Which sustains his relation to the nontruth of truth, perhaps?

That he should attribute it to woman, and to a movement of shame that would lead her constantly to veil herself, can only make woman laugh. The only thing that hides is what appears/disappears. And, when you get right down to it, she has nothing to hide. Nothing to show or show off that she could lose. Nothing to show or show off. From this point of view, she escapes castration.

And her game, with regard to castration, is always the game of "the woman" and "the man." It has to do with the veil or the sheath that she represents for him, with the envelope that she gives him to help him, sustain him, provide him with a doubling in his operation.

To avert the threat of her potential wiles, the daughter—while still a virgin—must be carried off into the territory of the father, the god. With one female forced away "from herself" in this way, and deliberately isolated, the other is always searching for her/self in order to touch her/self again. In this way she is constantly becoming everything that presents itself to her. No longer distinguishing herself from whatever is nearest. Which may amount to whatever is farthest—and "from herself"—if that is what what is imposed upon her turns out to be: veils, masks, in which she is concealed. In the very heart of herself, if that is what dominates. She is taken over by proximity.

That's what makes it so confusing—the distancing in the nearing, or the opposite. Which does not, simply, amount to its "operation." She, somewhat in-different, and from what is nearest to her, through excess of sym-pathy. But between her/them the obstacle intervenes that sets apart, and thereby deceives.

The cunning of the father, of the god? Rape/rob the female one so that the other can indefinitely produce doubles for him. Take the female one for himself so that the other, all the others, distractedly, may continue with the same operation but to his advantage. Multiplying his property. Indefinitely.

The exile of woman outside herself leads her to engage in inexhaustible mimicry to the father's benefit. Her death—that she grounds, doubles, but which is only the form of that which withholds her from "herself"—amounts to making her double anything, to the point that she confuses it/herself with it, loses it/herself in it: the abyss. Forcing her, by approximation, to cover the whole horizon of space-time: the space opened up between her/them in which her reembrace is always concealed. All discourse: repetition, but at a distance, of "nature." Replica that has already been mastered. She, sliding beneath, over, along, against, through . . . , those evidences or appearances that are empty of herself/themselves. That always wander aimlessly, floating, fugitive, lost . . . by nature.

By nature? Don't forget meaning which is to be understood, which has the sense, here and there, of something like:

When we love a woman, we easily conceive a hatred for nature on account of all the repulsive natural functions to which every woman is subject. We prefer not to think of all this but when our soul touches on these matters for once, it shrugs as it were and looks contemptuously at nature: we feel insulted; nature seems to encroach on our possessions, and with the profanest hands at that. Then we refuse to pay any heed to physiology and decree secretly: "I want to hear nothing about the fact that a human being is something more than *soul and form!*" "The human being under the skin" is for all lovers a horror and unthinkable, a blasphemy against God and love. Well, as lovers still feel about nature and natural functions, every worshiper of God and his "holy omnipotence" formerly felt: everything said about nature by astronomers, geologists, physiologists, and physicians, struck him as an encroachment into his precious possession, and hence as an attack— and a shameless one at that. Even "natural law" sounded to him like a slander against God; really he would have much preferred to see all of mechanics derived from acts of a moral will or an arbitrary will. But since nobody was able to render him this service, he *ignored* nature and mechanics as best he could and lived in a dream. Oh, these men of former times knew how to *dream* and did not find it necessary to go to sleep first. And we men of today still master this art all too well, despite all of our good will toward the day and staying awake. It is quite enough to love, to hate, to desire, simply to feel—and right away the spirit and power of the dream overcome us, and with our eyes open, coldly contemptuous of all danger, we climb up on the most hazardous paths to scale the roofs and spires of fantasy—without any sense of dizziness, as if we had been born to climb, we somnambulists of the day! We artists! We ignore what is natural! We are moonstruck and God-

107

struck. We wander, still as death, unwearied, on heights that we do not see as heights but as plains, as our safety!" (*The Joyful Wisdom*, sec. 59)

Nature can be loved only if she is concealed: as if in a dream. No sooner do they sense nature than the men of yesterday and today climb high onto the roofs and towers of fantasy. They are born to climb—to rise up. And feel not the slightest giddiness provided their climb is concealed from them. These night-walkers by day, these God-struck ones, these moonstruck men with eyes open, see nothing in it but art.

Their dream: to cover the natural with veils. To climb ever higher, get farther and farther off, turn away from nature toward certainties that they can no longer even see, as an escape onto dangerous heights— their plains, their plans. As a way to rid their thoughts of the disgusting things to which nature subjects every woman (?). Impatience, contempt, when their soul brushes against those things that seem to encroach upon their possessions: hands profaning their ideals. Deafness, horror, when faced with anything that is no longer covered by a skin, ultimate foundation lent by art in which even a pore would be impossible for lovers to accept—sacrilege in the eyes of love. Aversion to the sordid sides of the natural: blasphemers, assailants. Failings of ethics, of aesthetics, in that which the lover intends to bring back into the realm of the willed and the arbitrary.

But since no (wo)man can render him this service, he ignores nature, and lives as if in a dream.

The lover's day dreams attributed to the woman. What women want is: the concealment of nature. Moving away onto heights that elude the repulsive things about love.

There remains: the abyss. And then again. . . What if he fell. The tireless travelers to the very rim reach the abyss. Sudden drop off the plat-forms of certainties, risk of emerging from the heights-depths, of sliding off an artistically draped cliff—fall of the dice. Dizziness threatens, once again, God's tightrope walkers: a dizzying something that might withhold itself or give itself out to be. . . The boundary that crumbles. The ornament that falls to pieces. The mask that drops.

If that happens, blame it on woman as an encroaching indecency, an inconceivable dis-tance. And wrap her/oneself in imperceptible veils, raise her/oneself to the skies: moonstruck quest, for God. "Beyond the difference of the sexes, the ideal" which, at times, is made flesh.

A deep and powerful alto voice of the kind one sometimes hears in the theater can suddenly raise the curtain upon possibilities in which we usually do not believe. All at once we believe that somewhere in the world there could be women with lofty, heroic, and royal souls, capable of and ready for grandiose responses, resolutions, and sacrifices, capable of and ready for rule over men, because in them the best elements of man apart from his sex have become an incarnate ideal. The intention of the theater, to be sure, is not at all that such voices should create this notion of women; what they are supposed to represent is usually the ideal male lover such as Romeo. But to judge by my experience, the theater regularly miscalculates at that point, as does the composer who expects that kind of effect from such a voice. Such lovers are unconvincing: such voices always retain some motherly and housewifely coloration—most of all when they make one think of love. (*The Gay Science*, sec. 70)

The most powerful effect of women: to double for men, sublime souls. To give body—and with no difference—to their ideals. And as those ideals are the gods of the language: to give them voice, foundation—material for transcendental productions.

The empire of the word cannot do without the ear and the voice if it is to reproduce itself. But those still fleshly mediums are to be left to woman. Who, since she doesn't understand much about truth, faithfully doubles the ante, always adding to the pot.

The risk: those body organs can take over as they are taken over. Unless the woman is sublime, an artist in truth. The perfect doubler, faultless mimic, lossless game. Indifference achieved in faithfulness to her lover. Ready for magnificent sacrifices, not the slightest flaw in her conduct. No emotion that has not been mastered, perhaps? The music of Ariadne: at last beyond immediate pleasure and pain.

An exemplary echo chamber. An enclosure, sealed off of course, for admirably appropriate resonance. A physical setup that goes into vibration, amplifies what it receives all the more perfectly because the stimulating vibration comes close to the system's "natural frequency"—that is obviously constructed as a function of a model. A labyrinth whose internal cavities are always already limited, directed, speculated for the re-production of whatever should come

109

into it. A simulacrum without a hint of deceit. A theater from which every trace of decor is absent. A machine, that lets none of its design show, no part of its technique out, gives nothing away about its workings. Nature—remodeled with no appearance of manufacture, no deceiving intervention. There isn't even any more need to cover over, paint, dye, mask. Ariadne would at last have nothing underneath, nothing inside, no more depth, split, hole, chasm, abyss. She is infinitely divided from herself.

Her secret: she is all in webs. She spins all day long, all night long. And never undoes. The woman of your dreams. Perfectly absent "from herself." She—dizzyingly down in the nothingness of the natural world. Echo—but unique, solitary, tirelessly repeated, charmingly caroled, nightingale echo—of the master's words and desires. Wholly in the air. Giving herself endlessly out to be—be for him. Eternal—without body. Pure mechanism.

Hymen perpetually at stake, always shy of the moment of reckoning. Always and never virgin—without difference. Beneath the veil subsists only veil. She is still too ignorant or already too skeptical, for pleasure.

What do men want? They are left with the operation of the attraction that gives strength. Getting up close so as to be doubled, move away, or be exchanged. But she, infinitely outside herself. Marvelously far away.

The abyss, with nothing in store. For stores is what the master attributes to her, whereas that "elevation" comes down to his horror of nature. Henceforward, if he does not keep his distance—and depending on whether he has attributed distance—he is seized with dizzyness before this fathomlessness: dis-tance with no possible relations. No lips, since they too now, whether open or closed, beat the time, mark the tempo for distancing to take place.

☆

The woman, the idea, the female one becoming the other, the other the female one—according to the attributes given them—becomes transcendant, inaccessible, seductive. But if the void is the highest point for her, she drags everything down with her. "By herself." She fulfills the desire for nothingness. By playing with, acting the figure of death. If in fact she is acting. But so much is attributed to one who has nothing of her own. The risk: nothing is left. Erase that, by asserting that this was only a game. Then—the restart, the repetition, the recurrence—perhaps not in a simple way. Is she giving herself? Or giving herself out to be?

And in this "giving oneself out to be," what is kept of the self-giving? Does he give himself? Or only out to be? To what end?

Once the phallic show—what he has kept in reserve—is over, the question must be taken up and reconsidered. See if the process of taking over would still be master even to this point over "the unceasing war between the sexes," "the mortal hate between the sexes" . . . . For the affirmation or annihilation of difference, perhaps?

Once those envelopes/wrappings of ownership values fall away, reconsider how self-giving might sub-sist—between the sexes. Since the current exchange rate is perhaps no more than a semblance on the inside of sameness, a passage from same to same. Which explains the need for disguises: cut between the male one and the other—the other of the same, that is—which would manage to establish relationships only by means of disguise. By an extra layer of dissimulation: that is loaded upon the woman. That the female is reduced to.

Femininity lends itself to this: takes on everything attributed to or imposed upon it. Is it anything but a place of substitution between? Substitute, a vacant blind or canvas for productions and reproductions. May counterfeit—chance. But is in the end only a machine constructed by the iron hands of necessity.

> And if you want to conclude from this: "so there is only one realm, that of chance accidents and stupidity?"—one will have to add: yes, perhaps there is only one realm, perhaps there exists neither will nor purposes, and we have only imagined them. Those iron hands of necessity which shake the dice-box of chance play their game for an infinite length of time: so that there have to be throws which exactly resemble purposiveness and rationality of every degree. *Perhaps* our acts of will and our purposes are nothing but just such throws—and we are only too limited and too vain to comprehend our extreme limitedness: which consists in the fact that we ourselves shake the dice-box with iron hands, that we ourselves in our most intentional actions do no more than play the game of necessity. Perhaps!—To get out of this *perhaps* one would have to have been already a guest in the underworld and beyond all surfaces, sat at Persephone's table and played dice with the goddess herself. (*Daybreak*, part 2, sec. 30)

This perhaps would therefore—perhaps?—be fulfilled while playing at dice with Persephone. While taking the risk of laying bets with the woman from the infernal abysses. Far beyond all surfaces.

The thread is lost herein. The voice? of life and death? is lost here.

Persephone. The suspension of etymology. The fracture—in herself? in itself?—of the name, with no submission to a source, an origin, an ancestry. Passage that cannot be pointed out in truth, that is no doubt unnameable, univocally indeterminable, of the daughter —from the mother to the father. An operation of deflowering?

Ambiguity serves to cover her/it up. And in a different way. The suitor is supposedly the brother. But the mother's brother, or the father's? Through a complication peculiar to divine genealogies: brother to both. But it will be rather from the father's side that he puts himself forward. Property, in fact, can be held only by the males of the family. As a piece of property, Persephone belongs to the men. But the division of the patrimony has resulted in private fiefdoms that divide the brothers, separate them, and destroy common interests. Death and life have become their respective lots. Irreconcilably. The distance cannot be overcome. Particularly since the lower brother's inheritance would have the value not only of underground realm but also of abyss.

Ambivalence as to the possession of the earth, of the mother, which is doubled in Hades. Henceforth invisible, and with no possibility of encountering his brother on high.

Man, infinitely far away from himself, within himself, through the —impossible—appropriation of the mother. In order to bring him close to himself, between him and himself, the exchange of the *Kore*. But this operation demands dissimulation: they may no longer see each other. The high and the low, the heavenly and the hellish, the light and the dark, the truth and its other side, the reality and its shadow—can no longer meet. Giving-receiving no longer has a place between the male one and the other. Any bond between them must be masked: relations have a place only in secret.

And doubly so. The daughter who has been kidnapped away from her mother, from herself, by the father, is taken by the brother, the father's other, despite/without his consent. The *Kore* is given by the heavenly god to the infernal god, who can take her only by raping her. She is robbed, raped, robed, a second time.

This is the way with exchanges among man/men. Take possession, make use of, use up. With excess spoiling the object. The bonus that overturns value: virginity. Which—among man/men—is nothing more than the dissimulation of the product and its testing. Really taken away from nature is: the mother's daughter, and the nearness they shared. Man makes his approach, but factitiously, because of this rape and the gap opened up between the women. He transforms the need or the desire for nearness into an exchange value-wrapping.

The *Kore* has allowed herself be seduced, dragged off to her ruin, out of ignorance. Flower and fruit—so attractive for her because they were still "natural"—have got tainted with the power of resemblance. The end of the young girl, torn from her mother's arms, carried off into death, because she stopped to look at a narcissus, tasted a pomegranate seed. But she did not know the properties of these analogies. Was taken by surprise, in secret, for lack of knowledge, technique, of the semblance.

Dragged off into a world that to her is alien, she cries out. But no one heeds her. And her mother, though she hears that rending cry, is unable to find out where the girl disappeared. No living thing will tell her.

Persephone—the voice snatched away to death, with no trace left of the kidnapping. From *Kore* to Persephone, the passage must be forgotten. From her to her(self) there must be no possible connection. Between the naturally virgin little girl and the robbed/raped woman—paralyzed in her becoming when she falls into an abyss alien to her: death for the men—the intervention of a pretense, of a semblance of femininity, would seem to prevent any turning back. The female one should never remember the other. Once she has entered this world, she is never to return. Never cross back through that invisible veil that holds her, that shadow that surrounds her, that death that encircles her. That she grounds.

Her dissimulation? Her price among man/men. She is supposed to stand still, without tearing that hymen that covers over the bloody blow that must come to mark the boundary of ends: harmony, a pretence of harmony, between necessity, will, and luck.

Persephone does not stand still. Hence the risk of placing bets with her. The "perhaps," sometimes, finds its term there. The game, sometimes, is unmasked—the bounds of the sport. For Persephone knows all the plays. The highest and the lowest, the fairest and the most gruesome, the decoys and their realities. She passes, cease-lessly, from the (male/female) ones to the others, but she knows their differences.

It seems a woman alone goes from the darkest to the most sub-lime of the divine. Moving along the thread and then back again, without ever forgetting the operation that made her familiar with those abysses. Transgressing—again and yet again—the rupture, that nevertheless has been consummated, between proximity and property. The "will" of mother-nature and that of the father. Be-tween living in the increase of abundance, its rapture, and the law that allots property, determines its ownership, puts meanings and names to it, freezing its "natural" becoming so that, always already standardized, it produces, reproduces, re-produces itself. Prosperity is mastered, from its very source. No longer left to the rhythm of the seasons, for example. Enslaved to an immutable measure, to a fixed rate.

By knowing both worlds, Persephone—and without seeming to scorn her lot—will spend twice as much time in "natural" rapture. Her springs and her summers. The necessity for this, dictated by Demeter's refusal to produce anything if separated from her daugh-ter, her other "herself," leaves only the winters for her to spend with her spouse: the cold season. Carried off, far away, away from herself, ruined, Persephone becomes the ice being. Truth of any production that has been cut off from the natural world. Henceforward enslaved to a mirage technique that separates her from herself. Veiled with-out within, the *Kore* is arrested in her becoming. Immortally and never more a virgin.

In art, that perspective will again have simulated her, painted her, contrived her to suit an optics that is not—perhaps?—that of her "physiology." Which makes her—perhaps?—still absent from it. Makes her not have a place there.

In order to know, make a bet with Persephone. But that means—perhaps?—to risk seeing the end of the game. For she knows all the rules, and more. And can open up what one believed was the horizon of ends. Persephone, in effect, does not hold to one (male/female). She can sub-sist with different ones (male or female).

Of the woman who is artistically concealed, she has experienced the power and the charm. But she knows how much these last owe to the passage through death. More than Athena, who was never a little girl. Than Ariadne, who has not known Hades. Persephone has experience of the two veils, the two blinds, the two edges, the two cracks in the invisible. And the to-ing and fro-ing between the (female) one and the other. Crossing ceaselessly, aimlessly back through the frontier of those abysses. From below and from on high.

And if one were to interpret her "ambience," perhaps that would entail another physiology of art? A *"new* plurality"? For which the perspective would not necessarily be "the fundamental condition of all life" but that which, already, mummifies life.

Since, in some measure, *Kore*-Persephone escapes perspective. Her depth, in all its dimensions, never offers itself up to the gaze, whatever the point of view may be. She passes beyond all boundaries. Withholding herself from appearance, even without Hades. Whence the veils which she is supposed to cover herself with so that she may give herself out to be—what she is not.

She doesn't hold still in any simple way. Except as an—inorganic —mechanism. If she deceives, it is because this show doesn't suit her, cannot manifest her. Even if she were to wish to be wholly assimilated in it?

But because, through the reembrace of her lips—both passive and active, experienced without ressentiment—she still remains familiar to the other, she is disposed to receive him again and yet again into her. She does not take him *into* her. The other is not, here or there, taken into the whole of herself. She "wills" herself only with the other. She takes endless pleasure in ensnaring the other. Always moving inside and outside at the same time; passing between the edges, thriving in the depth and thickness of the flesh as well as she does in the farthest or nearest reaches of the outside of the universe. She goes and comes, in herself and outside herself, ceaselessly. According to at least four dimensions: from left to right, from right to left, from before after, from after before, the threshold of the inside to the outside of the body.

Thus is ceaselessly engendered the expansion of her "world" that does not develop within any square or circle or . . . and remains without limit or boundary. Anything occurring in that world is wedded in movement, if it remains an other that self-embraces. Passive and active, feeling without feeling ressentiment. This rhythm, barely

115

perceptible even to "small ears," sub-tends, nourishes, and accompanies others, like a background of air and light that is neither heard nor seen in and of itself. Bathing everything in light and warmth without appearing to do so. Tactile substrate destined to be forgotten, when the eye and the ear alone wish to marry/make merry.

The place of her affirmation already moves beyond and stops short of appearance, and has no veil. It wafts out, like a harmony that sub-tends, envelopes and subtly "fills" everything seen, before the caesura of its forms and in time to a movement other than scansion in syncopations. Continuity from which the veil itself will borrow the matter-foundation of its fabric.

This affirmation, without subject or object, does not, for all that, go to the abyss. Except in the case of someone who cannot perceive or conceive of her except as the "profound essence" of the Dionysiac. But there is no essence without the will to force her back or reduce her to being the relation to a unique mother-nature.

In her, harmony ceaselessly crosses back over the limit of the outside to the inside of the male one. She always puts at least two together. Not two units, but a two that passes from the inside to the outside of the ones, with no cut. An immediate mediation that is never represented, never exposed as such. Not that it is covered over with a veil, even in appearance. When the appearing (l'apparaître) is made manifest, she may still draw from it what she needs to mark the folds, seams, and dressmaking of her garments and dissimulations.

This duplicity of the veil has perhaps never received her interpretation. It is content to stick with what covers, masks, defers seeming (le paraître). With what already, in certain of its effects, lends itself to more secret diffusion. But it is in some measure sent up from the bottom.

Yet, without that flesh, while still in the instability of its life, all forms and all things risk being frozen in the icy rigidity of juxtaposed pairs, opposites, vis-à-vis, of resemblances or differences that are perhaps fertile in their relationships, still productive but lacking in harmony.

For such music, the passage between has to open, not just to crash into barriers, even if the barriers are interchangeable. Not just to meet appearances closed in, at every moment, upon themselves.

That move across their borders only to take possession of some "thing" of the other's, or even to take (back) all she has. Wedding ring that closes around the other he doesn't manage to espouse, as if she were his prey.

In order to make marriage, there must be a harmonious passage from external to internal, from the interior to the exterior of bodies. One arrives at the other without violently breaking down barriers, without jumping over the river, without being carried brutally into the abyss below or on high. Let the two be here and there at the same time, which is not to say that they are indistinguishable.

☆

Ariadne? She who bears a perfect resemblance. Faithfully reproducing the perspectives suggested to her. Who never holds them fast in any truth, except the one imposed in this way? Who has no strength but the one breathed into her and that she cannot keep. Unless it is for . . . ? And even then. . . In the instant, she is reduced to the mortal inertia of a double?

There remains that which does not simply yield to a vision or a question: her/the *voice*. Here the bonus that is resource for all the appearances. By this fact, her song always remains as fair as the first time: passage of life into the universe of resemblance.

This femininity, thus perfected, is deceptive. And multiply so. Life gives itself, gives itself out to be—a male other, and adapted to male perspectives. Ariadne—double of the male. Reproduces nothing that isn't masculine. That he should will himself to be also feminine doubles the ante perhaps. Doesn't change the game.

Unless you argue that "physiology" is the same for both sexes. A notion that covers over certain natural horrors, conceals them artistically. Giving rise to intoxication, the beyond-the-self, the over-and-above-the-self, the excess of life. But all derivative. And arrested in the truth of the/of a same. Limited. Even in its dizzy rapture. The drunken pleasure of being more, while remaining the same.

Which will be attributed preferentially to woman—the male's double. Whose operation is rather to double "within herself," without frame or term. Increasing, without end(s). Blurring every quarter.

But, in her, this perspective will be lodged or projected: self-identity. In this way, she would be the privileged trustee of the secret of the truth—and of her non-truth—in that she serves to constitute the identity of the same. But that necessity would be unveiled, in her, like her/a mechanistic fate. Her passage through/within a matrix that determines life, sets a pattern for the world of the senses according to *one* perspective, while subordinating them to a dominant value: the "ambience" of the masculine.

With any luck, any so-called fortuitous meeting, taking place within the parameters of this will: the permanence of the identical to itself. The fulfillment of this quest? All being machined to reproduce, without anarchy or obvious mastery, that end.

All being? Therefore woman too. Who is not only a female one— the risk. Beneath all those/her appearances, beneath all those/her borrowed finery, that female other still sub-sists. Beyond all those/ her forms of life and death, still she is living. And as she is dis-tant —and in "herself"—she threatens the stability of all values. In her there is always the possibility that truth, appearances, will, power, eternal recurrence . . . will collapse. By mimicking them all more or less adequately, that female other never holds firm to any of them univocally. Which suits the master as long as she goes along with all his impulses, agrees to all his measures. Faithful to himself in all her infidelities, she keeps her "ambience," while allowing him to move away and come back—opening a space between him and him(self) —following the demands of the becoming of his power.

Thus, it is she the ever mobile who gives him the possibility of movement by remaining, but just for him, the continuance of his being. Truth or appearances, according to his will of the moment, his appetite of the instant. Truth and appearances, and reality, power . . . she is—through her inexhaustible aptitude for mimicry— the living foundation for the whole staging of the world. Wearing different veils according to the historic period.

She mimics, equally well, the whole. For her operation is to double. But "within herself," and endlessly. As pure growth, she becomes whatever is proposed or imposed upon her. But under all those/her blinds, she sub-sists. Still. Each of those/her patterns— including that of being—is already blurred as soon as she appears. She is stored up and held in reserve by the very fact that she gives herself therein, but already and only gives herself out to be, in her "natural" development.

If she ruins herself in this way, it is because the airy wrapping she is clad in does not suit her. In this way, she deceives, and deceives herself, split between this becoming "of herself" and those mutations of form, those changes in perspective, those revolutions of the sun, that she weds herself to. Without having any stake in them. At least not simply.

And if the latest fashion is to will that she be phallic, she will prove to you that she is phallic, that you are right to believe it. Piling it on, until the phallus, and all the rest, go to their ruin.

Since, of course, all the perspectives that have already been fixed, all the shapes already outlined, all the boundaries already laid down, appear to her as merely a set in a game. That will entertain her— perhaps? But only for a moment. For as long as it takes to feel the limit, and start her operation again.

Unless she has been dead since birth. An immortal virgin, because never a little girl. A flower hypostasized into truth, appearance, semblance. . . According to your (votre) will, the necessities of your power, the historical moments. Everything at the same time, every woman at the same time, in order to please you.

Stop, dead stop, without end.

# WHEN THE GODS ARE BORN

# the child still in the cradle

The god lacks boundaries, limits—a skin. Conceived by the father of the gods and a mortal, he has experienced generation in the womb of a living woman, but not the slow maturing that builds a body in a dark nourishing soil before it comes into appearing. Dead before term. His mother reduced to ash by her lover and his thunderbolt while she was still carrying their child. Before being in the world, already born twice over. Already a survivor. He owes his existence only to the care the creator-destroyer takes to being his creation to the light of day.

Always already exiled from the place that gives him place. Always already wandering and deprived of his sustaining environment. Deliverance by a woman in labor is a thing unknown to this hybrid infant. Unknown the passage out of her womb. And the doubling of their bodies, the difference of their boundaries—the coming into appearance in one's own skin.

Not one of these events ever took place in the epiphany of this man-god. Coming one knows not whence. Always in the process of arriving, always in the process of appearing. An advent that happens over and again. The beginning again of an endlessly aborted beginning. Surging out of the abyss. Rising out of the deepest waves. Suddenly, in a great din of silence and death.

Thus is born the god of desire. He will have place everywhere and nowhere, inhabiting nothing. Revealing himself with great immediacy but then immediately removing himself from sight. Here and not here. Here—dead. Except for a mask that allows him to subsist. A frozen expression that prevents him from holding any one expression in particular. As soon as he is made flesh, he withers away. Any appearance suits him, and none. No sooner has he entered into one than it turns into a sepulcher, and he abandons it. The only skin he knows is a dead skin. And anyone who offers him her body to dwell in suffers the most extreme violence and survives only a short while.

This man-god survives in drunkenness. When he is not going back for refuge in the darkness of the great depths. Where all believe him to be dead. Whereas he is arranging his renaissance. By day, he shows himself only under a mask, and in ecstasy. Outside of the harmony of a body in which he cannot linger. Forever either higher or lower than the element in which incarnation lasts. He is endlessly incarnate and disincarnate. His appearance lasts no more than the wink of an eye. Made of light or of sound, wave strengths, no sooner spotted than gone. Always arriving, never coming. Refusing to come close for more than a moment: the moment needed to implant himself in a body and go off again, carrying away/leaving behind the appearance, tearing off/covering over the skin. When he touches from close up.

But, more usually, he works at a distance. Reaching from afar. Touching—from afar. He penetrates just short of or just past the skin, and never stops at it. This divine lover remains a stranger to all embraces. And he erupts onto the scene with blows. He opens, or reopens, and sets flowing. Suddenly loosing the flood in an ecstatic advent. Unchaining all that was captive, breaking the bonds. Entering with a great din, yet in silence, and cracking all the seals on the doors. Persuading everything to wander along behind him, spurning all dwelling places. Forever in motion, when he is not asleep. Going and coming, present absent, never where one thinks he has got to.

And his only sustenance is that brought him by his nurses. Who surround him, like the woman's womb he is said to have lacked. Endlessly giving him back life, setting him endlessly back in the world, wrapping him in that damp warmth that he never knew. Watching over him as he slept, waking him. Taking constant care of him—as a child. Drunk with his miracles, dancing with him, raving with him, yet never shedding their reserve. Warm, but also cold.

The man who has left a living woman's womb too early needs an eternal entourage of mothers if he is to survive. And all of them are his lovers and his followers, and his servants. And, for him, they would kill their own child, and fool the godliest of women, and commit the cruelest acts, for they are wholly devoted to his madness. To their love, without love. To their wild rapture. To their pure passion. That is sustained and intoxicated by its lack of fulfillment.

And to kill, rend, devour scarcely living flesh is a sign of their boundless desire. In their god's experience, is the first skin not the risk of death? Was it not necessary to slash open the womb that bore him so that he might not perish? Was it not necessary to open up the dead woman so that the living seed could be plucked out? Did she herself bring him into the world, that first earth? That closed space struck down by the father's thunderbolt, and his lightning alone will still split the hardening crust. Miracle of divine power taking the place of the mother's birthing. Annihilating natural becoming in order himself to give birth. Rebirth—after a first death.

And no longer devouring his son, but killing the mother, and cutting her up so he can remove the child. So he alone can ensure generation. The regeneration wherein the original murder is erased.

There remains the frightful abyss of a first event that is forgotten and remembered at every instant. The life snatched from death, torn away from the immemorial peril of an earth made sterile at the very moment when the fertilized seed already nestles within her. Torn away from a body that gives you life and then death. No sooner do you begin to dance for joy in the womb than that home of bliss is destroyed. Falls down stark dead. How is it possible to know that the father's fiery blow is the cause, when you are inside that original inhumation? Inside that cold and burning body that holds you, grips you in its icy sepulcher and threatens to consume you in flames.

And the thunder crashes, and the ground opens up over the abyss. Horror without memory, that yet never ceases to recur. And within the din, a silence of death. With the speed of lightning the lifesaving father rose up. Twice-born son, what a victory this is over the dead woman!

But the suffering is not forgotten. The perpetual torment goes on. And the terror remains. And the absence. And the pain of wandering begins in the destiny of the man-god. Who survives within and without a body. Having already experienced both life and death in his first home, and been already forced to leave it for a light and fire that were too strong. Shaded by plants, while waiting to bear the emergence into daylight. The father provides a shelter of dark and wintry leaves to replace the womb's sheath. Before birth, there is already the beginning of exile from the environment of a living skin.

And, for a god, he will always have too much the appearance of a mortal; and, for a man, too little the look of a living being. He appears in too much and too little skin. He changes endlessly, and holds still only under the mask. Motionless, and frozen too large. A face already set in an exaggerated expression, and not a constantly mobile countenance. He is still, and is not still. He is believed to be there.

And, behind this effigy, he looks you right in the eye. He casts a spell, by means of his very absence. An effect that covers over what is kept back.

This god of appearances stays within no limits. No sooner does he touch them than he is elsewhere. And he is never to be held onto in depth. That depth remains as if unfathomed. It can be taken for the abyss. That must be overcome by drunkenness. In the dance and in the hunt, he finds his footing again. Intoxication is his ground. All he wants rises out of it instantly. For him the solid crust is too hard and unfeeling.

And did this lover not suffer from the fate of his mother? Was there no pain in being smitten by thunder and split violently open? Rent in the most intimate part of his body in order to draw from it again the source of life. The flow of blood? And when his mother was closed up in the coffin of death, and disappeared into the under-ground world, did he not suffer with her? Don't these happenings make up the duplicity of his world? As he goes endlessly searching in the abyss for the object of his first love. Wishing to be reborn in his first birth? But always bringing absence back with him. And the absent (female) one.

For the chasm was dug, and hell created, before the child-god came into the world. The earth already conceals the mother's mur-der. The depths already pose a threat—as a reminder of crimes, obsession with ghosts, horror of disappearance, danger of revenge. The father's savagery, buried, covered over. The all-powerful lawgiver established in flames. The original already has no more place. Al-ready it is peopled with monsters in its depths. Sapped as other. Subjugated by violence, and resistant to the power of the sovereign gods. Subjugated and fallen.

The man-god is pulled apart by two worlds. His desire goes end-lessly from heaven to hell, from hell to heaven. He dances over their separation as if on shifting ground whose boundary he remembers and transgresses endlessly. The fire of the God of gods is deposited in him and he shows forth its power and cruelty—sending forth thunder, struck by thunder. Already one with Olympus and yet vic-tim and rebel to its order. Revealing this disorganization and the abyss on which it is founded. The horror veiled by its serenity. Powerful, like a god's son, suffering like a mortal. And unable to tear himself away from the memory of the dead woman. Calling endlessly for her, and wishing her to be reborn in Olympus. Returning also to the underground home of Persephone, who was carried off by Hades.

Celebrating dead women and refusing to consecrate the break with them. To forget their tragic destiny. Exhuming the chorus of the Erinnyes. Their rage, their shrieks, the whole together, the whole of them together. . . Raising the chorus to life again only to destroy it once more. As if a fatality or a desire dwells in him. As he loves the dead women and assures their revenge? As he loves the dead women? He in whom the power of thunder is vested and who exercises a power that kills? All at the same time. Between two births— mortal and Olympian. Still and forever a child.

Childhood of the man-god between the death he receives or gives, and the immortality of the gods. Revealing the pain of that sharing, of that passing between which soon will be cut off and erased. Buried. And, so that he can overcome the wrenching apart, surviving in drunkenness. That is derived from blood, from milk, from wine. Drawn from the well of superabundant nature. The intoxication of glory is not yet enough for him. Still too near to the original earth, and already so far away. So little present when he is here. An appearance in exile from his living generation. Already the descendant of an immortal.

The gods are not visible. They make themselves known without showing themselves in one countenance. When they allow themselves to be perceived as a face, it is already the choice of a mimicry. They are here, and not here. Presence that goes beyond appearing in a body. They appear unexpectedly beyond the space and time of mortals.

The gods are here. Where? When? Where and when no one expects them, even if one never gives up expecting them. Popping up instantaneously is their habit. Tearing through the world as constituted by mortals and a necessary support for it since they dominate nature.

By exceeding or falling short of the original harmony, the gods unbalance or rebalance the whole. Tearing man away from his early element, calling him beyond, driving him to ecstasy in the impalpable they inhabit. Founding the abyss that henceforth will inform all representation. But emptying the visible of the sap that brought it into the light. Cutting it off from its roots. Drawing it away from its dark maturation. And in place of its depth, its fleshly energy, substituting the fire of the spirit, of the soul. Of the supernatural. The gods set themselves up as the cause of the flowering of the living being whose organism thereby receives, within, an outer motivation.

Operation lost to memory, possession from the outset, rape forever covered over by a transcendental mechanism that transpropriates the growth of the vegetative. That gives a destiny to all becoming: plant, animal, human. The whole illumined and overcome in a will to achieve the divine beyond. But the moment of taking possession is a time of fearful crisis. Of convulsions, spasms, rending, multiple hemorrhages, earthquakes, screams, death. Covered over by the blinding flash of the lightning and the crash of the thunder.

Immortality is grafted only with horrible pain. And if man thereby receives an excess of light, the intuition of the world beyond, the contemplation of higher realities, is this not a return to him of the gaze that he sacrificed to the gods? At odd moments, like a lightning flash, he senses something forgotten, a vision no longer native to his environment. A heavenly viewpoint is rejoined. His eye catches glimmers despite the layers of obscurity he has wrapped himself in because he despises the eye that opens onto the world around him. And he sees, far away, a bit of blue sky.

Fascinated by the gods, man gave up the use of his eyes to them, did he not? In favor of a present that is not of the world, that is buried under multiple eyelids. Whose properties multiply infinitely. An accumulation of wealth whose power strikes down or unfolds infinite clouds of dreams.

He who withholds his gaze from each thing each day so increases the sovereignty of the visible that he goes blind. He who does not expend his strength as he goes along makes his strength into a power that can annihilate him. And the father of the gods, who does not foster the slow maturing of the living seed by continually giving body of his own body but who rather looms above and soars on high over that creation, enjoys a prodigious ascendancy. Potential held back, whose discharge breaks the harmony of everything that is becoming, and maintaining itself in the permanence of its living becoming.

In Dionysos, the fight to the death between two conceptions of the world is still staged. He participates in both, and clearly shows he is torn apart by that double allegiance. Discord that he overcomes only in drunkenness. Into which he draws all who follow him and share his suffering. Ecstasy that prefigures immortality but refuses to quit the earth once and for all. Preferring to die again, a violent death, rather than yield prematurely to the raptures in the natural world. Returning again and yet again to shelter in the great depths of the sea when the danger is too great, rather than seeking a haven in the sky. Disappearing, feigning death, but surviving in the duplicity of his destiny. And clad in animal skin, rather than divine appearance.

But he has already received the father's fire and refuses to let it serve only his Olympian blood line. Prodigal son. Too potent and impotent for the universe where he finds himself. That he throws into confusion at each of his appearances. At each of his festivals. He bursts on the scene in a way still and already no longer tolerable. His crazy desire loosens all bonds, destroys all homes, overthrows all institutions, laughs at all stability. Lets out what is already walled up. Sets flowing all the water that is frozen into solid walls. But he batters and wounds everything he opens up. And as he frees the fluid energies, he fractures the place they flow out of. As he lets the springs leap up once again, he annihilates the place from whence they come. By recalling desire, does he not destroy the body?

Implacable duality of this intermediary between gods and men. As he gives life back, he gives death. And the love he brings to life is already the love of eternity. The passion he inspires, a longing for death.

This monster already intervenes between body and soul. Making the one remember the other, and the other the one, moving ceaselessly from the one to the other, unable to settle in either one or the other, lacerated by their division, endlessly pulling down the barrier between them. And when he breaks in among the living, is it the (male) one or already the other he is searching for? Is it blood or soul he thirsts after? And might he not find his rapture in confusing the two?

And he suffers from the advent of two different natures, from the cruelty of the alternative, from the terrible way the sovereignty of divine power is engendered.

But he does not survive long. And when he is put to death, isn't this a show signifying his only possible future? Replica of his murders? But has he not lived death before he was even born? Where is the first cause of his destiny? And isn't the aim of his appearance the necessity of his disappearance? As a tragic act that has already taken place is performed under the mask, and is resolved in a divine cast of characters.

The child is born twice. Or perhaps three times? Isn't a double repetition needed to establish the permanence of the gods' time?

Conceived in the womb of a mortal by the god of gods, he did not mature in this original nurse. Is he saved from being doubly swallowed up? Saved first from a primordial nature that might have held him back from any differentiation, second from being devoured-assimilated by the father who immediately repossesses his product and takes back from the mother the property deposited with her. Conceived in a body, prevented from germinating in that soil, he receives his appearing from God.

It will no longer fall to the mother to say "yes" or "no" to the birth of a living organism, to let it out or hold it back. The fire of the father has taken this power away from her. Leaving her either impotence or the refusal to bring anything to the light. By making her into a crypt that is never opened, and absorbing into the night anything that lingers there. Still fertile and already sterile. Does she not hold back in the abyss everything the father does not take away from her chaos?

Would this be the way man sees the originary world that remains impenetrable to him? This the appropriation of a first nature, that resists appropriation. Taking place before any possible mimicry. And is not the mystery of a beginning, before his creation, increased for man into abyssal night?

Master of the daylight, the father no longer devours his children. He keeps them as a place where his power can be manifested, transformed, transfigured.

Dionysos still suffers from the earthly attractions felt by the God of gods. Still lover of mortal women. A necessary passage, until it can be annihilated. Seduced and seducer, he casts a spell in order to destroy—make the passage beyond. As he bewitches the whole, does he not discover a primary madness that summons an other order? He goes into bodies in order to empty them of substance, drink their blood, change them into divine longing.

At times he is already content with just music and dance. Suspension of his dementia? Dissimulation or sublimation of dementia in art? Unless music and dance were to lead him into new quests. Balance? Unbalance? Both. Or all three. Between earth, heaven, and hell, trying to put the whole thing back together again with no divisions.

But the primitive whole is already destroyed. And Dionysos shows more sign of mourning that disappearance than rejoicing in a new harmony. The child-god seeks again and again the way back to before the division and always comes to grief against the contradictions already in place. They tear him apart, and he carries and receives life and death at the same time. And as he returns to the cycle of his nurses, his mother, his sister, in order to be reborn, do the blood and milk he drinks not carry him into an otherworldly state of intoxication? That food is already mixed for him with a fire which goes beyond the simply living. Which has already piled it up and stored it, thereby assimilating and transforming it into a power of beyond.

Dionysos stays a little while. Until this operation, and its effects, are achieved, and the single outcome it permits. Is he put to death as child or as adult? Animal or god? Both. Everything. This immolation, this final tearing into pieces, precedes his third renaissance. While still a mortal, he upset everyone by the violence of his desire and his pain. He must be reclaimed by the Olympian serenity. Reduced to impotence by the glorious Apollo. Taken away from the love of his mother, a third time. Myth and rite will remain as a record of this.

An earth covered with fertile birthing is intolerable to the father of the gods. He alone may give the day. He alone may procreate and foster growth according to his light. And wrap the whole in productions of dreams. The lightning is his. And henceforward it will sire all genesis.

And what once was seen will be seen no more, but will appear only as the result of a celestial illumination. And the festival of the flowers and the festival of the dead women are commemorated as one. Triumphal mourning for natural blossoming. From heaven comes down so great a cloud that every earthly shoot is covered in a veil in which it (elle) is/is no more. Housed in a tomb of godly aspect.

Between two appearings, the child-god survives. One is said to have been given him by nature, one was imposed upon him by the father. He disposes of too much and too little skin to be simply visible, simply perceptible. If you imagine you see him, you see only a mask, and he turns up everywhere and it is impossible to keep an eye on him. He blinds the mortal eye. Fascinating it from beyond the tomb, beyond the night.

And no longer sure where and when day takes place, he sleeps all the time. Except when the women call him, when his nurses wake him, when his priestesses invoke him.

And when he opens his eyes, what wonder and enchantment! Where is he coming back from? What is he looking at with his gaze torn away from the depths? Up from the abyss? Nothing. He muses, drunk.

He has just been born, is scarcely conscious. A blur is still his light. Still in the cradle. When he has got up, and his eye is steady, his charm will fall short of this world, and move beyond it. In an attraction of heaven and hell.

But he always falls back into sleep. His cult is the cult of awakening. And if choruses of women do not draw him out of his night with their song, he keeps his divine eyes closed. And makes the world wait. Still he rests. Then suddenly bursts on the scene, immediately incarnate, then fades away without leaving any trace, except disorder and drunkenness. But with no possible memory of appearances. Only the mask, the parodic mask.

The god forestalls all images and representations. He comes, embraces, leaves. Plunging back into the night. And the nostalgia of his passage is sung by the women who love him. And they dance and shout out the memory and the hope of his return.

When? Where? Which is the hour to wake up for the god who remains between two days? To which morning should he open his eyes, under what birth reveal himself? In what light take form? What aspect show forth? What countenance adopt? And if he is still to hold on to a little living time, must he not borrow disguises? And is that false show put on for the benefit of mortal or divine gaze? Whom does he hide from? From both?

The mask is double at times. Catering to two appearings—short of the human, and beyond it. Frozen face of a divine mimic still looming dark over a naked, veiled-absent body surrounded by, sometimes even giving rise to, a riot of plant life. What transformation does the arrival of the god bring to living men? What transfiguration of the natural world accompanies the sudden coming of the man-god? How does man accede to the divine? What are the signs of becoming god?

Since he is not yet a god, Dionysos shows the way. And one of his favored masks is the phallus. Carved out of hard wood, supposedly taken from the sea.

Mask of birthing? Supernatural birthing? Of desire? One already modeled by the law of the Father of the gods? Effigy of love among living men? Interdict of happy relations with mortal women? Petrified potency fished out of the great depths after the mother's murder?

Power that still shows its ambiguity. Phallic Dionysos gives drunkenness and ecstasy. Calls beyond. Sets absence within and between bodies. Desire becomes an exodus toward death, sign of its approach. Erection commemorating its fulfillment. A monument to crime in its cadaveric stiffness, fascination of a ghost that is/is not in the depths, evanescent rising of one who survives only in the anxiety of disappearing, in the terror of vengeance. The mask covers the whole thing over—in a format larger than life.

What strange images offer an introduction to the mysteries of the child-god. Epiphany-return of the archaic. Except—that which still belongs to the earth-mother now presents itself only beneath borrowed disguises. The powers of the earth only appear thus covered over. As they draw near, as they show themselves to men, they draw upon that store. Already far from the sensual immediacy that blurs the boundaries of the one and the other. Such immediacy is hinted at, hidden, under wraps that maintain distance.

The gaze is made flesh and keeps itself well away from the power of the touch. Already taboo. Face-to-face encounter of a terrifying immobility that is experienced as a spell. Contact, penetration between living beings, is stopped. That suspension comes back in the form of immersion in occult forces. Which stir, writhe, and stiffen in their stony spasms, in their excess of reined-in movement.

The thunderbolt is already in mortals. Who no longer move, but stare at each other from a distance. A meeting of mere facades, rapturous over the volume in which surface has its place. Everything sheds its reverse side, its contour, its texture. Is reduced to a film of appearance. Freezing into that which is put on display in the present. Outside of growth, outside of becoming, outside of life.

And this mask that has been laid over the natural powers is a shield that prevents them from bursting out but it also multiplies them by holding them back, at least for a time. End and cause of the explosion of their strength. Limit of the unlimited that can only be contained for a moment. Before it spreads out again in some other way. Borrowing other masks or reproducing in the invisible.

The spirits, the gods, the souls are already here. And their opposites: ghosts, phantoms, specters of hell. Taken out of their warm glow, the harmony and embrace of their unity, the profusion created by their touching and merging, the beings that are still natural give birth to such powers and such monsters. Between them henceforth will stand those generations that separate them. Between them, heaven and hell intervene, those ecstasies outside the becoming of living beings. When they come together, abysses open up between them. Present, they remain elsewhere. Close, they no longer join up —the indefinite unfolding of their caresses has become an immensity of space that they cannot cross. Stock still, they look at each other, and no longer touch, except with lightning.

The gods are already in mortals. Phallic Dionysos opens a passage for them. Accessible to the senses, he yet signifies distancing. The shock of his sudden coming already heralds a rupture with life. But access to him is still offered in a wild manner. And, as he draws man beyond, he returns again and again to nature pouring forth. As the god who comes, who arrives over and again, who is always being born, and still remains among mortals. His love and his hate have yet to be polarized. He still mixes everything up together.

He still loves women. And when the difference between heaven and hell has been settled once and for all, he will appear as woman since he falls again and again under the spell of mortal women. When the *mimesis* of divine generation has established its sovereignty, anyone who loves women will become a woman, and anyone who loves men will be a man. Unless perhaps woman desires and summons in man the divine becoming? This is how the difference of the sexes occurs in the view of the order that is coming.

The child-god doesn't settle for that yet. At least not uniquely. He still lives in birthing in the senses. His passion for the natural world has not yet ended. He still draws his sustenance from it. He still feeds on blood, on milk, on wine. He still looks to it for rapture. Hence his exuberance that cannot live or survive on images alone.

And his eyes are wonders that feed on something other than the crust of the visible world, his gaze still stopping short, and going beyond.

That child still feeds at the breast—a god still in the cradle. Noisily voicing his hunger. And his mouth is not merely a place of oracle. He eats and tastes, like his prophecy. That still feeds on flesh, fresh and uncooked in the fire of the gaze. Getting drunk on hot liquids, not on sights iced in the sun of the eye. As does his appeal, which is not satisfied only by appearance. And these doings are horrible in the eyes of the gods to come. A necessary passage, to be wiped out.

And that child still lives in the wet. The dryness of lightning awaits his maturity, which he will not attain. He makes far too prodigal use of the thunderbolt. Unrestrained. And by using it in a world that still loves water, he disturbs it and dissipates its stored-up power. It is not kept as the stroke that founds an empire. He still plays and tries out its manifold fecundity. He mixes it up with wine. . . Smothers the thunder by wrapping himself in ivy. Sets up, in opposition to his father and his brother, the love of shadow, and the summons of his first birth. Flowering when the sun is lowest. Choosing their decline for his orgies. Celebrating his metamorphosis in their opposite. Asserting how little he needs them. How much he is attracted by things that grow without them—taking refuge in the deep ocean when everything threatens him.

Or revealing already the wintry character of the reign that is coming to be? Both. Moist shadow that protects against the flames, or cold serpents with deathly venom. And still mixing the fertile and the sterile, and making it appear that fecundity is shared. And that fire calls out for coolness, that the wet can bring gaiety. And that to separate them is to make them into poison. That one or the other brings drunkenness. And that the desire that wills itself to be the cause of one alone has already taken its source in the other. Fire coming out of water. Tree taking root in watered earth, and constantly drawing its sap from the earth as it rises upward.

Yet if the life force already has two faces, what is the source of this duplicity? Is it not heaven that has sent down a generation that aims to supplant the first, and not wed it? Even should the god grant an increase of power and glory to the living man, if this is not continuous with his conception and his infancy, is he not induced to

135

die, rather than flourish? If nature becomes sterile on receipt of that gift, for what growth is one indebted to the god?

And any creature that has its place only in the splendor of the light bleaches, dries up, and soon perishes. And any creature that shows its presence in trees lets them sink their roots into warm, irrigated earth and doesn't just make them into a torch so that he can enjoy the great flames. Is that show more spectacular than the other? Is it not joy in destruction to watch something burn up in an instant that has taken so long to grow? And doesn't nature develop slowly because of the slow rate at which it draws sustenance from the ground? When something is found in abundance only in light-ning and thunder, what gifts does it offer? What has it annihilated in its passage? And when something lights up the world so brutally, what regions of shadow does it create? Since its movement is always sudden and single, never does it dissipate shadows, but rather mul-tiplies them. And makes night into searing shafts of light. Destroying the wholeness. The element emerging from the shadow imposes its lofty form, outlines itself as a unit, and cuts itself off from the harmony of the whole.

And what becoming is yet at hand for something that detaches itself in this way from the place that gives it existence? Distancing itself from its depth by coming into such great light. Covering over the secret where the origin of being was found. Subsisting in the sleep of forgetfulness. Surviving in a dream.

And what is the nature of the work of someone who creates with-out water? Isn't he depriving it of the resources for multiple appear-ing? And how many faces are still to be born in the bottom of the seas? The lightning freezes one for all eternity. Prevents it from ever metamorphosing again.

He who has received his definitive shape can take in stores and feed on them, but he never returns to the element where anything may still take place. In essentials, he is torn away from becoming.

The child-god never stays away too long from his source. Should one of his forms be in danger, he goes into the great depths of the sea to be reborn. And comes back in another form. And does not long contain himself in one appearance. Often he bathes in the abundance of the waves, thus cooling and moistening his skin that has been hardened in the sun, and the eye's sun. And it is out of the seas, the fountains, and the torrents that he creates, more than out of the fire.

In wetness the seed of living beings finds a fertile element. Not in phallic erection, its mask. Frozen parodic appropriation. Always under any surface, in the fluid depths. Short of any form that is already visible. Short of or beyond all erection. Sterile.

Except for the seduction in drunkenness. Involving ecstasy—outside the body. Summoning dance and music. Recalling and forgetting the flesh as it remains in the movement of its becoming. The rhythm is too fast and goes beyond the natural beat. Exaltation that tears away from the roots. Attracts one out of the self, upward. Finding a place high up, on the very peak. Coming up to it by moving away from it. Having no element but the one drunkenness opens up at the end of its surge. Always ecstatic. Always beyond one's own body. Always in exile from one's own completeness.

Freezing, as it rises, the living world around it. Calling for nearness and creating distance. And fascinating with its sudden transports. Miracles with regard to the natural: Dionysos soars up/pours out in feverish growth. Instantaneous raptures outside the self.

And for the one who invents rhythms and songs to accompany and escort such movements as they erupt and fall off, to make them into art instead of chaotic savagery, are these comings and goings anything but pain?

And how are their presence and absence to be controlled? The absence in the presence? The presence in the absence? Gather the two together in one time? And hide their alternations? Endure beneath the mask?

The phallus masks. And behind the god is/not. He is believed to be there. For him, isn't it all a show? His plenitude is not there. At least not yet. And hidden, preserved there, frozen in the permanence of a hard wood, are his incursions out of the fluid element thanks to which he is reborn endlessly. His phallic procession accompanies his coming. Part of his suite, and of his parody, among the many marvels of life. And the fluid is more of a support and medium for his power than the phallus. Well, river, sea, milk, blood—these are privileged forces in his birthing. And that which will become an all-powerful sign of fertility is still, in his case, an organ of destruction. Out of nostalgia for what blocks the return to such places, perhaps?

Sometimes bull's horns. Avatar that becomes his prey, that he himself captures and immolates, that he consumes and under which he was conquered and cut into pieces. Through that dismemberment the unity of natural enchantment is undone.

The genitor to come once more shows his power. The desire that is being imposed once more displays its terrifying aspect. The mutation taking place testifies to the abandonment of native becoming, of innocent infancy, in favor of a disquieting maturity. Of drunken animality whose wiles yet captivate the prey to be consumed. Animal avatar, taken on by the god, who recreates the living according to his designs. Nature becomes monstrous. It is peopled with astonishing gestations that undo the harmony of the whole.

Brutal detachment from the native country that is inhabited by the stranger. And all springs, and plants and beasts, move differently. All familiarity is lost when such wonders show themselves. Terror takes hold of the living. Is it a gift from heaven or a peril from hell that comes to them? Must they be ready to receive more or flee and go back to the primitive land? Anxious suspension of everything. Halt in the continuity of becoming. Petrified expectancy for the savior god to break into.

But did he not produce the night just so he could appear as salvation? And was this great upheaval anything but the sign that his power must necessarily be established? And does he not create hell so that every mortal shall cry out to heaven?

The god comes. And darkness covers the earth. Thick shadow blots out the sky. The ocean is unleashed. The earth shakes. And nothing is as it was. Everything stirs and congeals at the same time.

And let the master of such powers show himself at last. Let him take shape. Let a faceless empire cast its spell over the whole world.

The thunderbolt crashes. The god is there. Wrenching advent. All ingenuousness is forgotten and turns, fascinated, toward this new dawn.

And this is the beginning of the exodus toward the beyond. Life after death initiates the world. The word comes down from on high to start trying to distinguish good from bad, what the gods love from what they condemn. Distinguish heavenly or hellish phenomena. Other day and other night lighten or darken the whole. And the rhythms are modified, between two tempos. Olympian calm or underground convulsions quarrel over the movement of becoming.

And doesn't every landscape metamorphose? Who can still recognize the intimacy of his birthplace? Into his home the supernatural has descended. And everything is thereby changed. No more artless embraces. Mystery invests the simplest gesture. A day of reckoning, both brutal and too slow, is expected, feared.

And the same advent, always and never there, is repeated, identical beneath new affectations. The uniqueness of an originary lost site is transcended in the unity of a time that is endlessly heralded and never lasts—the arrival of the gods. And all things live stretching upward, summoned out of their immediate surroundings. And each man is separated from the whole because he thus reaches up to the sky. And between each and every man stands the void created by the presence-absence of the god.

Dionysos still blurs and already marks the divisions in the whole. His passage brings joy and sorrow. But the falling short and the reaching beyond still mingle their sources in him. This god shows a passage. And makes a transition disappear. Between earth, heaven, and hell. Between two conceptions of space and time. The conception of generation into a mortal body, and that of transfiguration into men-gods.

And already the plant world grows to his tempo, the animal world is roused by his passions. Even if he still finds shelter among them.

And already women are drawn out of themselves, and transformed into immortals. Is he still lover of bodies? Already in love with souls? Both. The transhumance of the one into the other. Which is possible only through ecstasy. Their mingling again? Attempt at alliance? In which one passes into the air and the other does not yet live.

And the joy of departure fails in the pain. Arrives in port dead. The rebirth out of the great depths is frozen in the mask. In the still, spell-binding beauty of an arrested movement. A suspended desire.

The element of the child-god is still women or sea goddesses. Much beloved nurses of his cradle and growth. Whom he gazes on ecstatically in his drunkenness. He needs at least three of them. Three sisters devote their lives to the child of divine stock. Servants of his cult accompanying his madness. Sacrificing to the twice-born son some little boy or other of natural birth. And flouting the queen of the heavens with their scorn. Entering into the exclusive desire of the father.

139

And beginning to roam. Starting out from the mountains, the women are worshippers of the phallus. Leaving their sea home far behind, they are caught up and carried out of themselves by their eternal betrothals to the god who is coming. And their desire becomes a chorus of suppliant women in exile, the convulsive rites and dances of women in a trance. And the throbbing music of the summons to a wedding that is forever deferred pours out of them, like a fluid that the women still breathe out but is already bent to the rhythm of the man-god and therefore no longer flows from them. Or between them. The whole thing is driven by the very cult of the phallic effigy.

Their madness is still visible. And their pain. The violence of their passions. Exasperated to the point of destroying life. Still wild, but a kind of wildness already inspired by the beyond. A wildness in which the women become impassioned, lose their wits, their energies, move out of their native element. In the grip of movements too swift to last. Between rhythms that find no passage, lose harmony. And they collapse onto the ground from weariness at the conclusion of their intoxication.

And by unleashing resources that have already been frozen by the established order, the women shake off their reserve and show the power pent up within them. That is expended in mere spectacle? And with the aim of purification. Since their desire has been exacerbated and brought out under pressure from the god, only to be restored to order? And order's necessary accompaniment— art.

Does the god already love them so that he can make them into a work of art? Or else give them back to their animal and plant life? Both? He indicates the passage. The transition. Of death. His desire still needs blood and fresh flesh, if it is to enter into immortality.

But the ecstatic embrace in which the movement of love is suspended would already be the manner of his passion. And the lure of women whom mortals may not touch. May not enfold in carnal embrace. Women who repulse their lovers with the snake rolled about their bodies, keeping them chaste—the exclusive cult of the god. Whom they call upon as their gaze wanders up into the ether, drowned in divine love. Head bent. Broken women. Flowers cut off, stunted.

Birth of the eternal feminine. Women enter into mime when the power of the man-god is at hand. The power of the mother and the goddess of love gives way to the nurses and female servants of the phallic cult. Whose only desire is for their idol. Forgetting their own desire in the paroxystic exaltation of his. Is this not women's nature? After the creation of the world by a God.

The god comes. Between mortals, he first creates the void. And the terror.

All perception halts, holds back. And even the breath falters. The advent of the void is upon mortals. Nothing is seen, heard, or tasted as before. Familiarly. Between all things falls an imperceptible veil. The invisible comes into the light of day. The implacable and the impassive haunt the living. And over all senses descends a great cloud that makes everything distant. And the birthplace appears a land of exile. How to touch today something that yesterday was near? That was an element one moved in without the obstacle of a strange distance now hidden in everything?

The void and the stone are within mortals. Weight rivets them motionless to the ground, and the airy longing draws them up into the ether. Too heavy and yet too light is their destiny now. The desert grows within them.

And today they can no longer see what was apparent to them yesterday. Opening up their eyes, they feel separated from the immediate that surrounds them. Opacity and insignificance cover and dwell in all things. And the gaze, closed to the mystery of natural growth, enters into slumber and weaves a dream garment that carries the whole far away from its earthly blossoming. All is shrouded in an appearance that gives it a more striking and glorious aspect. Beauty shines in the face. Is laid over the face, like the mask of desire.

Touched by celestial love, she is perfected into an immortal image. And the torment of life begins. She who once drank deep from the well of perpetual becoming wishes to receive eternal youth from the divine fire. Carried off from her element, then abandoned on the distant shores of the island where her body lives. Entering rapturously into the desire of her god, and falling back into the tragedies of mortal woman. And the man and the god compete and tear each other apart through her. And the (male) one still wishes for the other, and the other for the one. But the one wishes to gaze upon himself in the other, and from fountains, to make mirrors. From the water of becoming, to make a mirror to reflect his destiny.

The women from the sea will soon be immortal flowers. The god lures them on from beneath the mask. Tempting them to become visible from a great distance. To shine with a brilliance that halts the gesture. Remaining, in some celestial configuration, untouched and untouchable. Veneration alone is acceptable to them. And the cult offered to one who already belongs to death. The shadow of mourning already enfolds them, through which sparkles their splendor from beyond.

And, from the sea, they will soon have nothing but adornment. Queens carried off from their element. Torn away from their birth. Mixture of life and death, of becoming and eternity, but in which eternity must always predominate. And love is that which, by separating them from themselves, draws them to suffer such agonies that the end of their divine destiny is accomplished. And from him whom they adore, they receive passage into the beyond.

From him whom they give life, they receive death. If he is son of the God. For now the women kill the little children of simple mortals, in their madness.

And all are mothers and nurses, forming a ring around the divine child. And blood and milk turn into hymns and songs of glory. And they thirst for glory, more than for love. And they begin to clothe themselves outside-inside glory.

# the twin brother

The god is born on an island. The smallest, most barren, least prosperous of islands. No land wanted any part of him. A foreigner in all parts. Migrator, invader, coming one knows not whence. Multiple and unknown in his origins. Of uncertain genealogy. Another cross breed, perhaps? Conceived of the God of the gods and of the immortal Leto—the god's favorite.

And also: twin brother. Of a sister, who births him. Helps him out of his mother's womb. Twice he is brought into the world. A baby boy surrounded by women. Only son of a female kinship group. With the exception of Zeus, he is born in the shadow of the archaic powers of the divine universe.

But the maternal genealogy will be supplanted by the patriarchal order. The number of women continues. They change ancestry and descendancy, pass into the father's family. The feminine remains powerful but henceforth submissive. Except for Artemis, the undauntable twin sister? Forever virgin, she will not threaten the reign of Zeus.

The coming of Apollo inspires terror. His revelation to the other gods is accompanied by noise and trembling—enough to shake up Olympus. What conflicts will again ravage the universe?

But the excess and the pride they fear in the young god will become wonderment. Might it be that the softness of Leto, his mother, has tamed or transmuted the child's violence? Far from setting himself up as his father's rival, he is revealed as a son of the Sun—not striking with thunderbolts, not burning, consuming, blazing, blinding, but rather lighting, enlightening, shining. Never the All Powerful One in the sky, he is rewarded with brilliance, beauty, and wisdom.

And if the *cosmos* awaits him in silence and dread, when he appears he is greeted with cries of joy. The earth is covered with spring flowers and with the slanting rays of a rising sun. Island from which and over which a gold cloud spreads. Advent of a morning in which a new light shines. Splendor of a dawn, perfect from its first hour.

The child walks and talks from the time he is born. As soon as he stands up, he claims his bow and his lyre. In order to proclaim, as warrior and musician, the will of his Father. Oracle of Zeus.

Thus the time of Apollo is revealed: as a time in which the god speaks. His ancestress and the mother-goddesses used to give signs or send dreams. This mode of divination did nothing to stop fathers killing sons, and sons killing fathers. With no explicit law, agreed by both, they were unable to be together, live together. These would devour those, and the latter would mutilate the former. Hideous dramas in which any god-man would insist on being the first, or even the only one. Whence the dread aroused by the mysteriously secret announcement of the birth of this son of Zeus. Who, this time, would destroy whom?

Apparently, no one. The patriarchal chain of relationships is put in place. On two conditions. Which perhaps amount to just one? The oracle will henceforward belong to the god-men and will take a different shape. The mother, all the women in the family, abandon their divinatory practices, confiding certain secrets about it to Zeus. And the son, as soon as he comes into the world, is spokesman for his Father.

The divine power changes genealogy, changes sex. One kinship line submits to the other. No covenant in fact. A reversal of power. Another age begins, which is still with us. It is prefigured by the meek love of a mistress-mother, who gives birth to a boy of great gifts, notably the gift of speech.

This Apollo, who starts off as an adult, still appears with the antinomic attributes of celebration and war. When he comes, everyone feels like dancing, and the hero is inspired with courage and strategy. God of the lyre and the bow. Curved instruments that require the harmony of opposed movements. They can be strung and played upon only if opposing pulls are balanced. Pull away from the self and hold close to the self, draw outside of and pull back within the instrument's middle line—the play of these forces must be counterbalanced if one is to be a good archer or musician. The distance from the self, and within the instrument itself must be maintained in one frame if one is to hit the mark or charm the ear. The center must be held between opposing attractions so that each person and all things are touched at their most sensitive spot.

This is the god of the dilemma in which the mutual resistance of the parts ensures the movement's equilibrium. In him and by him the space-time of a duel is opened up and remains in suspense. Destinies face off but lead to no tragic result, and Apollo is alert to preserve tensions that produce dynamism. And stability. Rivalries find no outcome here. They are necessary to order: between gods, between men, between men and gods. Each remains each, but mediation exists: both horizontal and vertical. This son of Zeus walks, dances, climbs, moves up and then down again, ceaselessly. He keeps or creates agreement by overcoming one thing after another, and keeping different loci correctly spaced.

He deliberates with his peers upon Olympus, he communicates directly with his seer who will carry the inspiration he has received to the hero designated by the oracle, and the hero in turn will spread it to his followers. All these trajectories or transmissions are achieved at the speed of light or of sound. No sign or dream to be decoded or interpreted. Only a thought or a surge from the heart, revealing that the god is at work.

He generally avoids making an appearance, avoids showing himself to the eyes of mortals. The "Brilliant One" often remains faceless. The god of light and luster does not make a show. He looks more than he is looked upon. Penetrating imperceptibly into the very heart of the seer or the man.

Nothing, apparently, has happened, but in fact everything is altered. The course of events is henceforward directed by an Olympian decree. The way that the fabric of events has been torn up and pieced back together by this change in direction is not even noticed. Apollo's attractions work like a spell. Often at a distance. No violence can be spotted, no perpetrator identified. He who is affected feels other, but cannot usually put a finger on how he came to be changed. He may believe he himself is the cause of it, and not realize that the god has intervened.

The divine enters the world surreptitiously. No break-ins, no bloodshed. At least in general, at least not visibly or even tangibly. In this way Apollo establishes the Olympian regime which will rule over men by means of a voice that speaks to them from within. The empire of the Father of the gods is founded by a mutation in the nature of signs. The mediator par excellence between heaven and earth, earth and heaven, will henceforth be the word. The God's sovereignty is installed through the privilege given to the word over any other system of exchange.

But here the word is revealed as inspired. It is transmitted or received instantaneously. A contact with the senses in which the word sometimes acts by effacing itself. It is still gestual. Actual. Poetic. It is breathed out, commands, it moves by transgressing the instruments, passages, threshold of its verbal production and reception. And without dialogue. At least in most cases. Whether the god speaks or the man speaks to himself, the difference is not always clearly signified. The seer, no doubt, is there as a guarantee. Intimately linked to the oracle. His mind attuned to celestial designs. Pulsing in unison with the divine *pathein*.

At times, Apollo chooses to show himself face to face. He comes down from the sky in the shape of a bird of prey. Sign, accessory, of the god's coming. He lands—he is there. Not incarnate, but expressed in the figure of a raptor. That swoops down, soars up, comes near, flies away—always between heaven and earth. Also a mediator. Symbol of the messenger.

The bird comes close to the man who is drawn out of his sleep or his coma by a celestial intervention. The god comes unto man between swoon and consciousness. Moment of nonvigilance—access to a different hearing. Opening into the extraordinary. It is no longer a dream but a hypnagogic state. Still short of consciousness.

The god is there. Standing next to the hero, he remains invisible. Sometimes disguised, sometimes wrapped in mist. No one sees him, not even the man he addresses and calls by name.

This is the way his approach can be recognized though the man himself cannot put a name to it. He knows that the god is close to him. He does not see him and cannot give him a proper face. He only feels him and hears him. And as he faces up to this elusive presence, the hero does not hesitate to make a polemical reply to the person who is leveling reproaches at him.

If the god announces: I am Apollo, the man calms down, listens to the advice offered, receives a promise of assistance. He becomes obedient, even as the strength to fulfill the command fills his body and his heart. Vigor is breathed into some, sucked out of others; courage comes to some, terror to their enemies. All vaguely sense the celestial intervention, no one can point to it explicitly.

Indeed, the god has not unveiled his particular attributes. Unless it be in his summons and in the presentation by name? But certain goddesses act the same way with their lovers or friends. Such intimate complicity with mortals is not specifically Apollo's. What particularizes him can rather be found in the important role played by the voice that seduces and mediates between everyone and everything. Sometimes speaking silently from one heart to another, one thought to another, sometimes aloud. Just a few words, enough for action or for inciting to action. The transmission of the king's will by means of a word, that is Apollo's signature. And to ensure that word is heeded, there is recourse to music, to poetry. And, for the essential part of the god's art, to the Pythia.

A burst of light or a disguise, the god's most common visual manifestations, may accompany his intervention. Conditions of that which offers itself to the sight: light and appearance. Resource of the gaze in all its forms? Substratum of visible whole—in white, black, and gold. Never being held within boundaries but bestowing them all.

Does omnivoyance become omniscience? That defines for each man, at each time, his own shapes and the measure of his action. Individualizing each one and each thing—contemplating them in their distinctness and their relationships.

Movement that must always be begun again. Since mortals, their bonds, their institutions, are not immutable. And since the immortals also at this period are still motivated by *pathos*. Are, therefore, changing.

Apollo comes and goes endlessly. Striding out among men. Distinguishing and gathering everything together into a harmonious figure. Whereas Zeus relies on the thunderbolt, Apollo usually acts gently. Or at least he is supposed to. Particularly because he proceeds almost imperceptibly and his effects always seem beneficent.

And there are few who bear the brunt of his strength and whom he chooses to try their strength against him in combat. Could this joust with the god be viewed as a greater mark of favor than any love affair? Though equally adept at war and love, could it be that Apollo prefers a fight? Or does he distinguish between the two? Might antagonism be his favorite place? Wrestling with his enemy, his greatest—his secret—jouissance?

In disguise, or from the back, he strikes his adversary. Ever striv-

ing, in different ways, to pit himself against other men. Coming near
them, accosting them, invisibly. Reaching them, in one way or another, while escaping any contact? Even the contact of the eye. And
turning up in those states of excitement or numbness, in those moments of passage between life and death, when men, heroes, and
gods can be met with?

Often he reins in his passion, holds in his strength. Passing from
the brute blow to the blaze of light, from vision close up to hearing
far off, from voice to thought. But always with the intent to seduce,
and conquer.

The god moves away, comes close, always touching from a distance. More and more swiftly. The sun's ray is faster than the arrow
from the bow, but the thought of the god is sent out even more
swiftly still. And transmitted better from mouth to ear or from heart
to heart. The divine presence is mediated and generalized. Perhaps
soon it will only take place in and by the idea?

Does not Apollo's splendor already prefigure the splendor of the
idea? Still possessed of a bodily appearance, yet more and more
withheld from the senses. Radiant because it contains within itself
every potential way of overflowing. Beautiful—still inscribed in the
flesh and thus able to lure one beyond. Already sculpted from without and within to speak with measured restraint. Idea made of light
and sounds that will be attuned within the voice that gives enlightened counsel, that dictates wisdom.

In that time, the idea still manifested the two things it had at
stake: polemic and enchantment, the bow and the lyre. Could it be
that Apollo covers the one with the other? Though he excels in
charm, might his most fundamental act be warfare? But war masked
beneath such elegant, seductive forms that it passes unnoticed. He
closes each man up in his own skin, the body armor of individuation.
Separates these from those, holding all of them united in the suspension of rival forces. It behooves him to inspire everyone with the—
king's—will for good. The message is breathed through all the barriers, those of the body proper, those of houses, those of cities. His
reign will penetrate everywhere thanks to the voice of the oracle of
Delphi.

Men will not pass in one fell swoop from tearing each other limb
from limb to this Olympian serenity. Hence the contemplation of
the splendor of the body of the man-god. Hence the ecstasy in the

dream of the fair appearance. Hence the feasts in which music and dance let license run free, without forgetting the periodic necessity for combats refereed by the gods.

But the rhythmic system of Apollo does not involve the orgiastic rapture of a return to primitive nature. It always keeps things in control. It brings men closer to wisdom. It tempers extravagance by allocating times for expenditure—festivals. Ritual ceremonies of abundance, of fertility. Often preceded by purificatory rites: medical expulsion of the *pharmakos*, preliminary mourning for the hero loved by the god, sacrifice of offerings. Exorcism of excessive passions, before the celebration of the cult. A spell is laid to avert any possible outburst of the archaic powers of the earth.

Apollo sees to everything. Keeps an eye on everything. Shaping the whole, clothing it in a veil of light, serenity, dream. The god of speech dresses the whole—outside inside—in a fair appearance. Masks the whole in an extra layer of skin: the brilliance of belonging to the royal sovereignty. Primitive nature thereby loses its contrasts of rapture and horror, exuberance and sterility. The whole is always already wrapped in a protective membrane that isolates it from a return to the rapturous undifferentiation within one unique orgasm with that originary mother. Everything is separated from everything, each thing inhabiting and inhabited by a dream that takes and gives shape. The poetry of the god shines forth and covers the whole with a still springlike, still matutinal gold. Still close to the solar illumination, but soon melted down into words that will generate and maintain a new, a patriarchal, order. The sky will soon be solid bronze.

The textile resources needed to reclothe everything are still borrowed from lavish nature. Zeus draws his stores of power and science from the old maternal ancestress whom, little by little, he buries in oblivion, under the earth. He still consults her, but in order to take the oracle from her and to gather up in Olympus the seeds of dispersed power. She knows where the risk of becoming divine is growing, even when it does so secretly, to threaten the father's empire. He, however, is unaware of this. She teaches it to him, knowing, better than he does, the future of destinies. She hands her gifts on to him. Is this to avoid the horror of murder between fathers and sons?

Did she need to give up all her talents to a celestial kingdom in order to prevent those murderous relations among men? With Zeus refereeing the feuds and conflicts from on high so that he can put the whole back together again? Taking from the ancient earth mother, from her daughters, from the women who love her, everything necessary to control the whole and bathe it in the light and the glory of his reign.

There will remain, of these archaic powers, the uncontrollable need to reckon with necessity—*ananke.* The excess that cannot be reduced to the power of gods, of heroes, of men as they organize themselves in obedience to a new, a royal, order.

But, to put that order together in Olympus and under his scepter, Zeus is diligently, jealously, active. He takes as his own all women, those receptacles of past or future power: ancestress, mother, wives, sisters, daughters. By seducing them, loving them, making them fertile or barren. To the henceforth routine genealogies of mortals, he still prefers a divine generation that transgresses ascendance and descendance. Incestuous by nature, the God does not exchange women with just anyone. He takes them or keeps them in order to establish his own family (with the exception of Persephone, perhaps?). Horizontal ramification that covers the earth and whose verticality is made to defer to his sovereignty that transcends everything, everyone, every woman. On its way to becoming the sole power.

But, to achieve this, he needed to dominate women. And the number of his mistresses is too long to count. Whether closely or distantly related by kinship or alliance, he seems to prefer mortals. Perhaps because mortal women are easiest to dominate? Or because they can still give him their blood, their fertility, so that he can make it into a dream?

Those women he does not seduce, he makes divine—virgins in his suite. And his most beloved daughter, born of his voracious loves with Metis, woman of the sea, will have only one passion—to be her Father's thought. Thus the all-fluid becomes the basis for the intelligence of the God of gods. She is born of him alone. Forgetting the passage into him and into her of all he assimilated of the mother.

From each couple of the preceding cosmogony or theogony, this King snatches a daughter whom he takes for his mistress. Gathering up for and within himself light, water, earth, he rebuilds the world, gives it a new horizon. Looming over the world from his heavenly vantage point, with his look of thunder, he interrupts the mortal conflicts between male ascendants and descendants. The mothers, sisters, daughters, will have brought him what he needs to establish his heavenly dwelling. Their blood, their flesh, their love, their fertility are assisting in the creation of the sovereign abode of the Father.

Is not all that is lofty and sublime in him pressed out of the bodies of those mortal women who have been seduced by the all-powerful fire and carried away from their genealogies? Women who begin to separate from each other and within themselves through the incessant action and intervention of the order of the God. Carried away from themselves, far from their primitive strength so they can serve the production of the Olympian abode where the immortals dwell. Offering themselves or letting themselves be taken so the gods can weave the dreams they use to wrap themselves and clothe the whole world. But aren't men owed what the gods thus steal from women? Do they ever reinherit it?

Does Apollo, the best beloved of Zeus, dream of man or of woman? Is he an apparition of man or of woman? An artistic manifestation of man or of woman? Magnificence of man or of woman?

And whom does he love, if we leave aside his favorites? Does any woman shine with the beauty he shares with her? Does he give back to any woman the ecstasy, the enchantment, the divination woven from her flesh?

Even his ever chaste twin sister will become his dark and baleful double. Has shining Apollo not absorbed into himself her luminous image, leaving her only the shadow? She who birthed him a second time? He who is born of his mother and his mirror-sister? Born twice into the world? Twice into the light.

Product of a love of fire and ice. Merging the two in his single self. Yet never simply to be confused with one or the other. Son of the thunder, he shows himself as the god who appears as a blaze of light. No longer immersed in orgasmic fusion with primitive nature, but bursting forth in the splendor of an erect male body: reared out of the matrix of the archaic powers of the earth. Sculpture of a man carved out of the undifferentiated matrix of the earth-mother who has engendered him?

By doubling the father *and* the sister. Apollo—god of twinhood? No longer kills his male peers, but takes from his sister what he needs to establish sovereignly his identity. Gloriously insisting upon his singularity, by leaning upon the brilliant image of his female double. Advent of an appearing that has a skin of its own, even as it leaves the skin of the other in the night.

From the ancestress, from the mothers, sisters, daughters, mistresses, Zeus seems to have taken the fertility of blood, of flesh, and of all the cosmic elements, so that he could spin the gold of his sovereignty and the bronze of his heaven. Stealing them from within, taking them for himself as virgin-companions. Apollo, we might say, steals his sister's outer skin. Without touching it, without brute force.

Taking possession in the subtlest way—steal the appearance of the other in order to ensure one's own permanence through a doubling of skin. Apollo, it seems, no longer penetrates into women simply as a lover of their beauty, which he takes or assimilates.

The fact that he either remains invisible or shows himself only in disguise—not in drag, as far as we know—would be evidence of this floating between two skins. Of his wishing still and always to have the other's skin, so that he can enter definitively into his own. That is never simply his own. Whether disguised or materially manifest as radiant or diffuse light, or else as sound, he illustrates the quest to appear oneself, distinct from the whole. Endlessly unfolding veils of beauty that serve to figure the self-identity of the god-man— neither simple mortal nor mask.

But, ever dependent on some double, ever in suspension between the one and the other, in some measure like, this immortal adornment is intended to belong to one side only. Or: split into a shining and a dark image. To the resplendent man corresponds the fatality of dark woman/women. One doesn't go without the other. Right side and wrong side of the same operation.

This crime of fair Apollo doesn't show. No one catches him in the act of killing or robbing her. Only a thread running through the myths of his rise to power, only the backing on which he weaves the miracle of his advent and of his Olympian gift of measured restraint can be interpreted thus.

And he who entertains and realizes the dream of achieving peace in equilibrium, of overcoming the pain of living and of insoluble tragic dilemmas, also reveals himself to be the master of duels in which no violence breaks out, because one of the terms has been removed.

This son, for example, through example or excellence, does not challenge his Father, and is not devoured by him. But one piece is missing in evaluating the approach of this serene maturity: the duel, that has always already taken place, without any fanfare, between him and his sister. His twin's glory will always consist in bringing children into the world, bringing each one into his own skin. She, the virgin, forever rebelling against all constraint, impenetrable friend of wild beasts.

Because she endlessly gives their/her skin to others, leads them to wrap themselves in their/her appearing, irrevocably, Artemis will lack a skin. Subsisting between the animal and the divine kingdoms. Without an identity of her own, kept within ambiguity, leaning if anything to the ill-omened side. Except for the—glorified —need the city has that she be present at births. But she herself, a humiliated little girl, a forever chaste teenager, a forever loveless and childless woman, finds her place more in the camp of dark, baneful women.

To Apollo's blazing light corresponds the darkling fall of his sister, or her reappearance as moon. Neither twin maintains the level that was, at birth, his or her own. The (male) one passes beyond, the other falls short. The one rises up, the other is humbled. The one takes all the brilliance, of which the other is but a reflection. The one attracts boundless admiration, the other an unreasoning ambivalence.

What event took place that is never shown, in this creation of the god of light? What operation eliciting ecstasy—the going out from the self? What zeal motivates those faithful to Apollo?

His most secret conquest: to surreptitiously adorn himself with the grace of his twin sister. Just as Zeus swallows Metis the fluid-daughter of the man and woman of the sea so as to give birth to Athena, his thought, so Apollo takes into and upon himself the mirror that is his sister so that he can give birth to the dream of beauty. Being of fire and ice, for a moment he holds in balance the contrasts between thunder and frost, the too hot and too cold, the too immediately present and the forever distant. His glory still shines out, like the glow of a rising sun. But it dazzles so, without burning, that it must already be made of ice.

Theophany of the god of speech. Still cosmic, still of the senses. In which the triumph of the speculative is already heralded. This son, mediating the Father's will, prefigures the way the tragic will be overcome by the theoretic.

In him, those two worlds still remain in tension. Hence the wonderment, the in some measure mysterious wonderment, that greets this new god. But it takes the elimination of one member of certain pairs for the new order to carry the day: the twin sister protagonist. And, henceforward, she will be seen in the indomitable and warlike guise of a huntress who loves animals. Surreptitiously, Artemis will always already have served as *pharmakon*.

The city is organized, the new order comes into being. The renown of male gods on the way to resolving their tragic destiny begins to shine forth.

Obviously, Apollo is prophetic. Nothing yet is hard and fast. The time is at hand, this god is coming. In him, and through him, the future is sculpted. Can be seen in advance. Can be read as in a heavenly mirror. Can be heard from the mouth of seers. And this oracle still makes itself felt and heard in a kind of transitional state: between sleeping and waking. Not far from a dream, but beginning to take shape in meaningful words. It is still a matter of appearing and appearances, but the voice will soon cast a spell that goes beyond or falls short of the gaze, the world of the senses. What we see is interiorized and disguised: invisible or unrecognizable. Beauty and wisdom begin to dwell in language. Movement still animates the body and the limbs but already passes into speech—often having its effect at a distance. A mediation that touches without the god needing to come close in his incarnation.

But at this point, the game is not yet over. Spring and morning of the birth of a new divinity. Of a hitherto unknown configuration of the relationship of men to the supernatural, of the relations of men among themselves. In the gestures, in the words, there still breathes the amazement of a new dawn, the flowering of an unexpected spring. Nothing rigid, yet, nothing still. A time of incarnation for the divine in which man is moved differently, receives new inspiration, not as yet imitating something he neither knows nor recognizes. Alert, in a state in which dread and gladness, death and life, agony and resurrection, are mingled.

The prodigious thing about Apollo is that apparently the new does not kill the old, dawn does not imply twilight. The rise of another world seems to occur without the earlier one declining or dying. God of dream. . .

Because he masks the pain of living, the alternance of joy and suffering, and the implacable nature of the cosmological cycle, Apollo will be the most sublime of the Olympians. The god of transfiguration, within a certain forgetfulness. Offering initiation into the contemplation of the idea. Confidence in an immutable truth as supreme good.

The passage from the ecstasy of delirium or love to the ecstasy of philosophy is prepared with Apollo.

Who is unlucky in love. He is credited with as few mistresses as his father is with many. He is more usually met with in the company of men. Competing with them, seeing, admiring himself in them. Multiplying himself ad infinitum through them. Unfolding and refolding of appearances without end.

How does one break into a skin that has already been taken away? How turn back toward her whose image one has seized? How find one's way in the night, when one is only made of light? How touch something that has dimmed and faded in your dazzling rays? Unless it involves touching oneself again in pure appearance?

This god-son, friend of his Father and of certain of his brothers, often meets with infidelity from his mistresses. Are they not giving him back like for like, in compliance with his own economy? Since his version of fidelity is obscurely based upon a mime of appropriation. This beardless boy cares nothing for women! Unless he can steal new charms from them. He never competes directly with them, doesn't seek to move them, barely talks to them.

And how could he deal with women? Henceforward, for him, they are invisible. They are either too naked or too covered up. Only their attachment to some other god-man might make him remember that they exist.

Apollo's destiny isolates him from women. For them, there begins a period of abandon. A period in which the god-man embraces himself indefinitely through them, by the mediation of their flesh which is transformed into airs and out of which he creates his dreams or works of beauty.

In this excess of appearances that he borrows from women, in those endlessly multiplied veils, a body in the process of abstraction

155

is shown and is hidden. Apollo now touches himself only by means of films of light or dreams of ice, suitable stuff for him to weave the splendor of his glory. Flesh passing insensibly from life into the mere spectacle of life. That rolls and unrolls into brilliant surfaces that are not receptive or porous to love or desire. Unless it be of the— glorious—self?

Indefinitely built up of images, profiles or dreams birthed by the other, he is held frozen in his form or his statue, like a shell carved out of indestructible material. The immutable shapes of stone. Shell that gathers together everything Apollo has borrowed, halting any tendency to disperse, or pass back into the other or into the primitive orgy. Keeping him unique. Detached. Serene. In the end, sovereignly indifferent.

Love or desire of the same. In order to define and affirm himself, the god holds back, in suspension, impassive. Reining in his passion, he gazes upon himself and admires himself. And also those like him, among whom he remains the most admirable.

And if he prefers jousting to passion, isn't this necessary for the establishment of his power? Power reined in so that it can become yet more sovereign? This is not the time to let power flow out but to identify it in its form.

This god does not reach out to the other, is not prolifically fertile, but uses his strength to mold shapes until they are perfect. Between him and those like him, affairs are always subject to a higher discretion, and to the dance's demand that one maintain one's own tempo.

Rapture is no longer an immersion in the orgasm of an original nature, but an intoxication in an ever overflowing celestial mirage, taken up by rhythm in the strictly cadenced movements of the music, as well as of the body. Between the primitive orgy and the bliss of the dream, the (male) one is sought. No more effusion in the limitless unique, but creation of a dream that carries each man beyond—luring him into the love of the immortals, into his own ecstasies.

To reunite each man to the next: the word of the god-king. To organize the city, conflicts between favorites, and conquered adversaries. Hierarchy of elections. A radical reordering, veiled by the seductive charm of Apollo.

Which floats everywhere, barely perceptible. An ambience that enchants and comforts man for the pain of living. Everyone enters into their skins by forgetting them. Wrapped in a protective lining, in an armor, that isolates them from the communion of the flesh. Solar sons of the Father, shining scions of an ancestress deep in the ground, of submissive mistress-mothers, of dark twin sisters.

A single sex is measured and contemplated in himself. Sovereign conqueror, without a genuine duel. The other is remembered less. Except as muse. But usually she is left in the night. Hidden in the shadows or in the moon's reflection. Or else she is abandoned to the animal kingdom: wild, indomitable nature, excluded from the *polis*. Sometimes sacrificed to the gods or eaten.

Her only glory? To serve as midwife to sons and brothers of light, who own the gift of speech. To give them again and again that containing medium that is their/her skin so that they can be born of it and shine with added brightness because of it, without wholly losing a sense of proportion. The women are turned inside out and unfolded indefinitely inside outside so that those children of light may glitter. And the women will then be their pale reflections.

The life and death struggle between twins to take possession of the image did not take place. At least, not apparently. The (male) one doubles his own image, eliminating all difference; the other will subsequently receive the excess brilliance that has been diverted toward her, confided to her care. She becomes the negative of a wondrous apparition, the memory of its creation, of its stamp. Always ready to let him come into the daylight, to bring him into the world. Even if it seems that she must receive light from him— nocturnal star, lunar other.

But Apollo, in order to overcome his twin sister, moves away from his own body. Excess of light and glare, ultimately slave to the specular or the stone. Splendidly lonely. Touching only from a distance, even when he is near.

To make himself understood, he already needs speech. And he is not easily recognized since he appears in so many guises. If he fails to name himself, people often mistake him. And if a body is given him, it is a mineral body. Otherwise there is no getting hold of him. Too fleeting, volatile, invisible, he the god of appearing.

He bestows what he takes. Measures, shares out, separates, joins, according to the Father's will. A mediator who has borrowed from primitive nature what he needs to complete his operation. But that resource is neither acknowledged nor revealed, it is neither named or invoked under this new regime.

It was right to fear this god when he came into the world, right that no land wanted to receive him. Among all men and all women, he is the most subtle murderer. With one dart he can wound and kill. And even when still and silent, he coats everything, outside inside, with a brightness that is already icy. Paralyzing imperceptibly, from birth. Leaping beyond natural growth and bloom, in order to establish the kingdom of the word.

Could it be that women, and only women, notice? Attracted by his beauty, women would yet abandon him for one who still has a body of flesh. Knowing where he finds the source of his mirages. And preferring damp heat to the death of the immortals. Original intoxication to lonely ecstasy and, soon, the bewitchment by the idea.

Apollo—enveloping love and desire, making them less and less attainable by means of stratified layers of various materials, or their sublimation, exaltation in the air. The arrow and the word of the oracle alone still touch the heart of man. Cutting through all visible manifestations. Moving beyond or falling short of the skin. Of all skins.

This is how it goes with the instrument that kills. Apollo remembers the incarnation in murderous combat. He knows the strategy for destroying the adversary. And not just any strategy. It is no longer Zeus's thunderbolt. A still cosmic attribute which is made without the help of art. Here the raw material, whittled like dead wood, obeys only the strength of the archer. She has become a lifeless tool, posing no threat, were it not for the project of the god-man.

It is the same with the *pathos* of the oracle. No longer manifest to the senses as a sign offered for interpretation while remaining a natural phenomenon. Perceived only—within some realm of the interior whose relationship to touch remains to be defined—as the word or thought of the son of Zeus. The soul is decked out and made into a mere place of passive receptivity between "God" and men. A venue for the farthest distant to become the closest at hand. But what kind of closeness?

The oracle still uses music as a vehicle. The shock of force may herald him. Light hides him and hides in him, as well as in and under the sanctuary of Delphi. Rapid movement alerts him or draws attention to him. All these properties will soon be assembled into language, product of mortals. Is language received from the gods?

That would be the divine Apollo's message. The God will henceforth make himself manifest only in words. And the relation between men will soon be conducted almost entirely by means of language.

In the voice's breath might something of the flesh still persist? Something imprisoned in a body of ice or stone. Sealed into the tomb of individuation. A tomb erected, and twice set apart, from the place that gives it birth. Still aglow, already cold.

Speech, alone, sometimes still moves the soul. Gesture and place of communion between heaven and earth, gods and mortals. A living earth, inside the human heart, where man might relate to man outside of war. Among men, within men, they would now address each other without murder. At any rate father to son, or son to father.

Advent of a religion that fosters the establishment of the city in accordance with patriarchal sovereignty. Men are bound to one another by harmonious hierarchy. Now that they have become strangers to their primitive nature and are assembled according to the needs of a *polis*, with the gods' complicity. The extermination of one by the other to achieve the existence of a single (male) one has apparently ceased. A mimetic chain is put into place between fathers and sons, between brothers. An ever open chain—the imitation of the father, in order to annihilate his power as model, would no longer be operative. Attributions are shared out. The son participates in the father, according to a genealogy which leaves to heaven the sovereignty of the whole. Brothers trade off as their special characteristics dictate, but always with respect for an intangible empire.

Apollo does not exclude Dionysos. They complete each other in Zeus, but never reproduce his unity. Apollo hands down the celestial patrimony of the mantic, the light, measured restraint, justice, the organization of the city. Dionysos inherits his father's thunderous excesses, the gift of seducing women in drunkenness and ecstasy, the attraction for water, the possessive and devastating passion of night.

The two—couple of false twins?—must coexist as incarnations of the power of Zeus. Even if one surpasses the other in power, the division of possessions, here, cannot be closed. The whole will no longer belong to any one. It is up to the brother-men, without resorting to bloody warfare, to divide up the Father's attributes. Including those he has stolen from the ancestress or the mother.

159

Theogony mimics cosmogony, and parcels up the universe into properties in which each (male) rules over one part of the world. Which presupposes a whole politics of covenant. Concessions and rights must be instituted.

As for example between Apollo and Hermes. As was true of the couple formed by Apollo and Dionysos, Hermes unveils all that the god of divination keeps secret or masked: the ever enigmatic, dangerous, even lying or stealing character of speech. And, also, what fabrication speech may conceal. Hermes appears as the double who is more dark and wicked and who must be dealt with if the explosive, rending travail of rivalries is to be avoided. The two brothers will make themselves known as complementary. In the different ways they are born, for example. Hermes will be the smaller or the bastard. But Apollo, the legitimate brother, will allow Hermes to share all his gifts, short of giving up his constitutive privilege: to be the oracle of Zeus. Hermes, therefore, is deputed to transmit the Father's wishes—as these have been revealed by the favorite son— and to ensure that they are carried out.

Truth, for her part, remains alien to trade or division. One (male) holds her in check, unveils her, proclaims her. If she gives occasion for fearful contempt, the responsibility will fall upon the ignorance or the madness of those who receive her. Apollo may lead men astray. That does not affect the value of his word. Problems arise because of the eternally erratic interpretation of the oracle.

Between gods and men, territories are set up. At least in the no-man's-land of the heights of heaven, the depths of hell, and inside the boundary traced by the oceans. Dimensions installed by a cosmogonic trilogy that leaves each term in its generic place. There remains the earth ancestress, a fourth term, that was once the most fertile, that has been progressively buried and forgotten beneath the architectonic of patriarchal sovereignty. And this murder erupts in the form of ambivalences that have constantly to be solved and hierarchized, in twinned pairs of more or less good doubles.

These oppositions, concessions, subordinations between antagonistic forces reappear, endlessly, in couplings between gods-men. What remains in the night is the life-and-death rivalry between Apollo and his twin sister, which he masks underneath his sweet reasonableness and fair appearance. The fight and the compromises with the ancestress, the mothers, sometimes even the mistresses are on display. The brother-sister couple remains unresolved. Is this the deepest layer of the *mimesis* hidden in the night of truth? Might the most successful Greek creation seal away from the eyes of the world the way it uses mime, both defensively and offensively, in dealing with the female other? If Zeus acts like a mother, by giving birth to daughter and son, Apollo acts like a sister, by surreptitiously snatching the sister's qualities for his virile stature.

In this way the god-men may defend themselves from the archaic forces: with Zeus mimicking the mother, Apollo the sister, Dionysos the mistress? Even as they ensure the power of the masculine order, which they aim to keep. Extending it throughout the universe.

Mimicking the maternal-female role is equivalent to hiding it/oneself as other in the strategy for establishing the royal sovereignty. Inaccessible to those men or women who might take them as prey, the gods-men attract the love or the desire destined for the feminine powers and in fact, because of their kinship with women, they are able to approach and seduce people, notably women, without arousing feelings of dread or revulsion.

The divine son avoids being devoured by his father because he merges into nature. He harbors within himself an attraction for the female goddesses, and because he resembles them in part, he surreptitiously assimilates them. He will merely need to make himself known as a cosmic power—light—and seize from nature her musical harmony, or else veil his body in beauty, disguising it, dressing it up, invisible whenever art does not immobilize him in stone; or else, and above all, be birthed as same (comme même) by his twin sister.

This game of mimicry protects and seduces, and the third term in it would sometimes be mother-nature, sometimes woman-sister. By dissimulating, assimilating himself therein, or by assimilating them, he becomes them and they become in him. Mutation in which the difference of the (male) one and the other disappears for the advent of a unique kingdom—in a dream that carries us far from the pain of living. Unfolding between earth and heaven, heaven and earth, but neglectful of the subterranean abysses or the immersion in the chasms of the sea. Spread over the whole surface of the earth or slipping over the waters, without ever returning into those great dark, wet depths where shapes blur and blend. Borders, edges, that are guarded and keep each one in his delineated shape. Affording him a bonus of dream, musical rhythm, polemic, divine inspiration, speech, in which he can move without the erection of his own body being affected by it. The form can remain immutable. Remain fixed thanks to an excess of appearances, on this side and beyond.

Taken from the other are her depths and these are used to produce the beauty that, henceforward, extends between earth and sky. Ecstasy cast in the figure of Apollo. The man-god, twice birthed by woman. And who no longer falls back into the chaos of woman's womb. Keeping himself eternally standing. Effigy of a power that has no flaws.

Zeus's thunderbolt no longer strikes at random, except through his son Dionysos. In the case of Apollo, the thunder appears-does-not-appear in a constant light that continues to shine out between the excess of night and the excess of day. Scourge of an equilibrium between the too high and too low, the too hot and too cold, the too big and the too small, Apollo seems to announce the ideal power of man—erected between earth and heaven. Mortal immobilized in the contemplation of immortality.

So that life may be possible—Apollo, the god of dreams. A store for every kind of plastic form, brilliance that heals earthly weakness, prophecy that opens the horizon of an Olympian gaze. Sun, yet calm. Passionate perhaps, but never at a loss for charm. Emotion, forever held in check by a fair appearance. Always transfigured. Will to survive beyond all sufferings, since these are artistically veiled with an art that feigns naivety. Mirage as powerful as the horror inspired by nature. Call to be swallowed up in illusion, answering to the terror of the rending rise of life.

Apollo lures us into contemplation. Without a command, a reproach. Play of light and mirrors that attracts and holds us fast in the sublime. Drawing our attention away from the daylight and its contradictions, into an ecstatic vision. Constant need to be delivered by an enchanting appearance. Alerting us and transporting us into an immortal's zeal.

The natural scene finds its manifestation artistically captured in an otherworldly permanence. An Olympian beauty for which the body of the god will be guarantee and deposit. Rest for the eyes that

162

do not yet perceive and are unable to remain within the rapture of a heavenly radiance. Too enslaved by their customary mode of sensing to see that sight that precedes all sights—brilliance itself. For man, that sight would have to take on human form to be admired. That would be his measure: the limits of a figure.

And knowledge of the self, without the forgetfulness involved in excessive love or delirium. For him, therefore, Apollo—the god who splits, divides, separates these from those. Limns the outlines of the one and the other. And serves exaltation up to them according to a tempo suited to their powers. And no more.

# the crucified one

## epistle to the last christians

The son of Man is born in Bethlehem of Judaea, in a poor stable. He is brought into the world by a teenage virgin pregnant by the Holy Spirit. Begotten not made. In Mary, the word was made flesh. And God came among us.

This mysterious conception leads, first of all, to the repudiation of the woman in which it takes place. And then, as soon as the child of this miraculous event is born, he will risk being massacred by the king. Were it not for the intervention of the angels and of dreams, he would not have received life, or would not long have survived. And this son of the Word will enter into his glory only when he has suffered crucifixion and death.

How is this story to be interpreted? This testamentary narrative? This new pattern of relations between God and men? This Christic symbol that dominates the Christian era?

"The Word was made flesh and dwelt among us, and we beheld his glory, the glory as of the only begotten son of the father, full of grace and truth." (The Gospel of St. John, 1:14, in the King James Bible).

Word made flesh—does this mean it has come into a body that is forever separate from others, and from the whole of the universe? And that it will find communion with the whole and within the unique only through the sacrifice of his person to the Father? Must the individual be immolated if unity with God is to be achieved once more?

The coming of Christ, following on the time of Apollo, would seem to destroy the illusion of a life without horror. Open up the wound at man's heart. Claiming, as potential redemption, that passion and death can lead to the Kingdom.

The Christ thus makes manifest a new way to overcome the pain of living. Instead of the rapture of cosmic fusion invoked by Dionysos, he asks man to look to the resurrection through participation in

164

the glory of the Father. Dionysos, that slightly recalcitrant son of Zeus, sings, dances, draws every thing, every man, every woman into the orgy of a return to a primitive mother-nature. Apollo casts a spell over men through the oracle of the God of gods, leading them away from the original intoxication, toward another illumination, another cadence, another rhythm, a tempo that checks excessive outbursts, hinders regression into the infinite of the relationship to nature, masking his approach with dreams that simulate nature, thus maintaining a distance from the whole and between all men, wrapping each man in the beauty of his pose, the appearance of a proper skin.

The Christ would open up the walls of this tomb. Not toward the depths of the earth but toward the abysses of Heaven, not through or for the mother's passion, but by identification with the Father's Word. He would go from the Father to the Father, without a backward look at his birth into the body. Bridge between Life and Life, tying the end to itself, without beginning. Coming from On High, and returning there. Ring or wedding band that seems a new link to the earth, here below, but no longer marries/makes merry (ne fait plus la noce) with simple living beings—the dead. He comes from the Father. To the Father he aspires. Toward the Father he walks and never falters. By the Father alone he fears to be forsaken. Showing the path to be followed if one is to obtain transfiguration, resurrection, ascension—become the Father's Word, and accept agony and crucifixion as passages from incarnation into eternal life.

This is the most common interpretation, and in general the values of sin and redemption it espouses have formed the basis of Christian ethics. This Christic model consecrates an historic stage where man stands between nature and God, flesh and Word, body and speech. Moment in which man constitutes himself in boundless allegiance to the Father's will, and in which the attraction of the original mother, wife, sister, mistress disappears, even as enchanting reflections.

Not that women are absent from the evangelists' path. But they appear there as virgins or repentant sinners. Softer, more submissive than the mother of Apollo, they listen to the Lord's word, and it is enough to fill their cup with joy. Are they nothing but ears? With just a bit of mouth, eyes, and as much hand and leg as is needed to reach out and follow after Him. They seek Him, not He them. If He does occasionally take notice of them, it is out of his infinite benevolence, neither needed nor earned. Sex is virtually absent from their meetings, except for a few confessions or avowals of morbid symptoms. He listens, but does not marry/make merry with women, for already he is bound to his heavenly Father. At best, he takes part in some symbolic union that ignores, or defers to a time after death, the fulfillment of carnal exchange.

This is the Christ handed down to us by tradition. The tradition that reveres the wound in the side of the crucified one. In the body of the son of Man there reappears, in the form of a wound, the place that, in women, is naturally open. Also by and for him, perhaps? Doubling something already there, that is forgotten, covered over, buried, and is symbolically reborn, to signify the return to heaven. Does this mean that Christ takes upon himself, mimics, the female in order to effect the passage back and beyond that creature whose flesh constantly incites men to lose control. The threshold that in her crosses the boundaries of the body and gives access to the infinite becomes in him a violent, yet already bloodless, penetration, marking the passage into Eternity. All that she offers as an abyss of life and jouissance is closed off, like the mouth of hell itself. All the inexhaustible love she conceals for anyone who knows how to approach her is projected into the All Powerful On High. She, a dumb virgin with lips closed, occasionally receives the favor of a word, which she must bring into the world in the shape of a child of God. Mediatrix between Word and flesh, she is the means by which the (male) One passes into the other. Receptacle that, faithfully, welcomes and reproduces only the will of the Father. Grace that no longer abounds in her womb, even though it is from her womb that she will birth the child.

But as soon as she says, "yes," and without the slightest prophecy or herald, she also is "crucified." Before her "son" endures that destiny, and also afterward.

Such would be her participation in the incarnation, death, and resurrection of the Word. Obscurely, she is in mourning for belonging to the earth-mother and to her sexual body. This is her cross in life, this double closure of her lips, upon which is implanted the visible erection of his passion.

To the virgin who lives forever because she dies to her generation in order to become merely the vehicle for the Other, corresponds, in a sort of mimetic representation, the murder of the man she loves.

The man to whom she gives flesh must be sacrificed, in his living body, if he is to accede to a transfiguration worthy of the Kingdom. A second time, life is inverted in death, and death claims to be real life—Life.

A second time. But the first time is not noticed. Is forgotten as a condition for the—apparently—singular event of the second. All that is retained is the Christic figure, for whom Mary seems to be merely the instrument of conception in the realm of the senses. The "how" of that mediation is barely interrogated. The manner in which she has already lived what is repeated in him remains hidden. Or perhaps comes up again as necessity for a belief, a dogma? The Christian world cares little if the crucifixion is the echo of the annunciation—evoked at the same "hour." It celebrates a memorial and neglects the prologue or the prefiguration that memorial unveils and masks in the erection of its model.

Is this the force of the symbol, however obscure it may still be today? Is the tie binding Mary to the Christ venerated only in inverse ratio to its mysteriousness? Could it be that she is the "mother" of the Savior only because she is the first to incarnate the historic coming that he is? Or becomes. The double event of the annunciation and the crucifixion would, in fact, always be tied together. This virgin, indeed, is always to be found at the side of the man they call the son of God, like his female other of whom he would be the manifest reproduction. The matrix that engenders this man without a father remains invisible. The cross to which her lips are nailed is not revealed. She carries it secretly, buried in her "heart," like a silent sorrow, that does without religion.

But her "yes" subtends Christian culture, which would not exist without her. And if the nature of this *fiat* were questioned, perhaps the basis of centuries of Christianity would need to be reevaluated. Because, according to the traditional interpretation, her "yes" is equally a "no": a no to her own life. To her conception, her birth, her generation, her flowering. No to everything, except the Word of the Father.

All that is left of her loves and desires is the patience, gentleness, tenderness or compassion that, on occasion, she breathes into the ear of her "son." Reminding him, perhaps, of certain aspects or necessities, sufferings, or joys of incarnation? As for the rest, she follows the man before whom she came. She receives, from him, the

Word that she passed on to him. She contemplates, in him, her own work—of giving body to the divine presence. According to tradition, she will take him in her arms only when he is dead. During his life, she is there, but at a distance. And no man accompanies her: she knows no men. Physical embrace will be banned from this religion of love. Its only unions are celebrated between mouth to ear, sometimes with the gaze, always through symbolic mediations. Spiritual unions. Analogous to those consecrated by or in the *theorein?*

What, then, is the originality of the message? The public staging of something habitually hidden away? The model of *pathein* corresponding to the Word made flesh? The miracles of affection between a virgin-mother and the only son of the Father? The only one whose killing will be a public spectacle? The only one transfigured and glorified in the power (la puissance) he incarnates? The only one upon whom devolves the revelation of the Truth, the institution of the order guaranteeing that Truth, the first liturgic gestures, the thaumaturgy. . .

But this couple, of which one of the two always remains in shadow, recalls or heralds many others. Is its singularity to be reduced to the status of popular illustration? Accessible to all men and all women? Perhaps.

*Et incarnatus est* would mean the manifestation of a paradigm that henceforward is applicable everywhere. And that one epoch in history needed to trumpet abroad. Perhaps to push to its tragic perfection. The life of Jesus of Nazareth could be read as the last great founding tragedy of the West. None other, to this day, would overpower its pathos. Which is all the harder to interpret because it is not played out in any theatrical site. Its setting, its timing, its characters would be those of life itself. No space, no moment, no actors, no author, want to represent that tragedy as such. No work apparently. There is only a play between the forces of On High and here below, of Heaven and earth, of Truth and error, of Good and evil, of God and idols, of divine and human nature, of Life and its mortal errancy . . . of all those pairs of opposites that continue to tear the world apart. For the glory of the Word? Since the only presumed, imputed, or credited signature is that of the Father.

☆

Her work is therefore: the Word that creates heaven and earth. And that is engendered in the "Son." But what or who claims that the Word has been, and will forever be unique? Transcending the universe, ecstatic to the world, immutable throughout all ages? Beyond the transformations of cultures, of languages? Words of a people, certainly, but intended to be universal. What incarnation, including that of the relation to the divine, can thus be taken out of the world of becoming? Dependent upon a language that is eternally the same? With scribes, translators, commentators or priests being the only people able to decode a Truth that has been revealed once and for all. The only valid interpreters of a tradition that is forever fixed in a lawmaking text.

Does the "death of God" not mean, therefore, the end of the security lodged with, of the credit accorded to, those who thus suspend meaning in the letter? Those who immobilize life in something that is merely the trace of life? The preachers of death who paralyze the becoming of peoples? Those who indefinitely repeat the identical, because they are unable to discover difference?

*Et incarnatus est.* Must this coming be univocally understood as a redemptory submission of the flesh to the Word? Or else: as the Word's faithfulness to the flesh? With the penetration of the word into a body still recalling and summoning the entry of that body into a word. Exit from the tombs. Access to a beyond here now. Passage from body-corpses to a saying that transfigures them—pulls them out of the walls of their death. Crossing their own frontiers in a meeting with the flesh of the other. Living, if she speaks. She too incarnating the divine.

*Et incarnatus est* manifesting a different relationship between flesh and word. Approach into a touch that no longer drains bodies of their animation by the saying of them—either in acts or in words. Bonds in which human and divine are wedded.

And not just people gathering around some "Good News" which they expect will be repeated in the Parousia. Can the people hear its prophet or prophets? Heeding only the signs handed down in a testamentary Scripture. That proclaims or attests the Truth of the letter. Accomplishing the rites prescribed by the text. Mimicking the gestures the Lord is reported to have made. Each man striving to be like Him, in order to be pleasing to the Father. To become Him, in order to live again in God. Each man like Him and like his fellow— all united in one mystic body? Excess or dearth to the communion of the flesh? Effusion into something that, here, cannot be shared?

Or offering "in God" of a bonus born of the exchange that has been made? Action of assistance to a people in exile? Or place for the projection of the supplement of power for something that cannot be realized at the time? Both? In that case, what is referred to as "God" has nothing to forbid. The more his people live, the more "He" exists. And his glory would demand merely that life increase.

Which can be understood in various ways. As a fetishistic or magic respect for the tiniest, plant-like embryo. Not as a trace of the cosmic drunkenness that still sent men into delirium with Dionysos. This cult of the biological seed is no longer testimony to an overwhelming love for the mother, but to a fascination with the precious paternal seed that is dispensed into her. The mother-mistress can and must suffer, or even die—in silence moreover—in order to honor those chromosomes of the male race, that priceless *logos spermatikos* poured into her.

What Truth supports such a respect for life? The word made flesh? Or the power of patriarchs that works by the repression, seduction, and legal rape of the body of women who know the value of gestation and childbearing? That the growth of life might mean the proliferation, transfiguration, resurrection of bodies in and by their word is intended to remain a veiled or censored message. That the Christic symbol might be decoded as an invitation to become shared flesh, still causes an uproar. That "multiply" might not simply mean "make children" for the Father, but rather create oneself and grow in the grace of fleshly fulfillment, is sheer blasphemy! That God might be engendered in love, in a fertility that goes beyond and falls short of actual procreation, is an interpretation that the priests of the Messiah still seem unable to hear or make known.

How much do those priests understand when it comes to life and the flesh? So, "move on." Leave them to their opinions and their ressentiments. Search for traces of the divine in anything that does not preach, doesn't command, but enacts the work of the incarnation. Shun the temples, in order to become a living people. Liberate fleshly encounters from the taboos that pervert them. Leave the Christians to their crosses! If what they want is the hellish cycle of suffering for compassion, of wounds inflicted or sought in order to bring down the redeemers-thaumaturges, of bodily humiliation in order to believe in the resurrection, then, yes, let them have their "games." And open a new era. By reevaluating the kingdom of "God."

☆

*Et incarnatus est.* Does this presuppose *crucifixus?* Or has accident supplanted event? Negation supplanted affirmation? Death, life? Lonely agony, the invitation to sharing and to divine engendering in the incarnation?

For incarnation nudges us toward the deciphering of the function of that virgin-mother. Who is more ancient and more recent than the Father and the son. Who survives through the centuries. To whom an age must at last be given. A date and place of birth. A conception, a birthing, a childhood, an adolescence, a maturity, a death. A life. By unsealing her from her silent "yes." By giving her the word?

When are we to have an "Annunciation," an "Advent," a "Christmas" in which "Mary" is conceived and anticipated as a divine manifestation? Meaningless phrases? In part. But. . . According to Christianity, God is found only in Distance, the relationship to the Father only takes place at a remove and in the respect for separation. God—the Different, who is encountered only through death and resurrection.

And what if, for Mary, the divine occurred only near at hand? So near that it thereby becomes unnameable. Which is not to say that it is nothing. But rather the coming of a reality that is alien to any already-existing identity. Relationship within a more mysterical place than any proximity that can be localized. An effusion that goes beyond and stops short of any skin that has been closed back on itself. The deepest depths of the flesh, touched, birthed, and without a wound.

This divine is still to be revealed. Which doesn't mean it can never be expressed. But it is always aborted as soon as announced. Never expected or recognized in its coming into the world. Its incarnation. Which surpasses the limits of individuation—and without a wound or an abyss. Except in the idea that man creates of it for himself and imposes. When he imagines a virgin-mother conceiving by the Holy Spirit so that in her neither the uniqueness of a living cosmic dwelling nor the infiniteness of woman's jouissance should deprive the Father of his Will and of his Heaven.

But what is meant by the spirit? What is Mary listening to in the message of the angel? Only the Word of the Father? Or is she heedful of the universe that bears her, of a heaven and an earth that have always been and are still virgin of culture? And that, going beyond and falling short of the word, make its engendering possible. Woman-mother consubstantial with a nature by which the word is nourished and fostered. Since her sexuate body never separates from the place where it has place. Never is she folded back upon herself, except when the figures and names that encrypt her are laid down. Always in communion with the *cosmos* which she lives in and which lives in her, and shelters in her. Cradle of infancy in which what remains to be revealed can be sown, can germinate and come into the world. Some word still to be incarnated, perhaps?

Hers is a divine that does not need to erect any capital letter. Hers an omnipresence that pertains to no Person. Creeping through the mesh of any code of law, the nets of institutions, the organization of Churches. That uproot her from her most living source of inspiration. By assigning her a place in the religious scenario. As a receptive-passive female extra, not as a divine source. Flesh that has already become word beyond any locatable figure. The holy spirit?

Who listens to the annunciation that Mary makes? To the memory or the experience she attests? The excess to a certain God who speaks through her? The access to the divine that passes through her? She, required to be the Father's respectful daughter, nothing more. A chalice into which his love may overflow? She is constrained to deny, even to blaspheme her relation to the divine by allying herself with idolatrous representation, by participation in liturgies that consecrate a body and a blood that she has always already given naturally so that the Word might be made flesh. These rites make an economy of absence, consecrate disappearance, establish nostalgia and expectation. Of what? Or of whom? What Parousia is still expected by those whose Messiah has already come? A glory, with no agony, for the man-god?

What mourning for her is veiling the horizon of a return of the divine? And when she is bidden to adore a God whom she has no share in, does this not lead to playing the devil? By simulating a possible alliance within a male Same, by doubling a love or a desire that are not her own, she in fact splits the son off from his Father. Her mimicry props the whole thing up and covers its tracks. Carries the "way, the truth, and the light" into errancy or the labyrinths of hell.

"Mary" agrees to this game or doesn't. Is the bearer of heaven or hell, of life or death. Or both? How is she to be understood? Do the priests of ressentiment have ears for her prophecy?

Or do they refer her to that mythic beginning of the history of redemption? To the first sin of an Adam led astray by an Eve. A woman is, apparently, at the root of man's separation from his God. Already idolatrous? Doesn't "original sin" consist in dissociating human and divine? In making God into a distinct and transcendent entity. With the expulsion from the "earthly paradise" corresponding to the will to know God as such. To the desire to produce him as a "suprasensory" realty? God—Different? And this would be the source of evil, in the beginning. A sin against the incarnation into which woman would lure man? Eve would incite the being she was created out of to reveal himself as God?

The myth of the earthly paradise, in her version might it not be interpreted as a memorial to existence "in god"? Once they were "in god," with man and woman sharing heaven and earth. In the midst of nature. Feeling no need for any shelter but a garden where they lived naked. Obscurely living a desire whose cause they did not name. In the perception of a divine that was not opposed to them, perhaps? That was not even distinct from them. Neither representing nor knowing itself—having place in their midst. Then God did not exist in front of or above human beings. He was in them as they were in him. This "they"? A man and a woman, an "original" couple. Before what is called the fall, or sin, or banishment. The "outside of"—god, the earthly paradise, the relation between him and her, her and him.

How does banishment occur? In the mode of the "being like unto God." The position of God as model to be repeated, mimicked. Thus, set outside the self. Surely evil, sin, suffering, redemption, arise when God is set up as an extraterrestrial ideal, as an otherworldly monopoly? When the divine is manufactured as God-Father? As long as the divine remains within the human as its strongest center of attraction—in the midst of and between the man and the woman, according to the myth?—would either fall or redemption have any meaning, except as a way to forget the deepest or the most intense

173

aspect of the attraction? God living on, aware of and faithful to the forces and tendencies circulating in the universe. Gathering himself in so as to share himself out and perpetuate "creation" in nuptial celebrations among those attentive to the whole? In alliances in which human and divine are invited to wed. With no store of "supra-sensory" knowledge to separate them from the innocence of fleshly communion. Banishing them out of the most intimate part of their destiny as mortals? Driven out of the "garden." Destined for the errancy of guilty desires, dwelling in bodies that henceforward are masked or veiled. Allotted different tasks and punishments: toil for him, and for her the pains of childbirth.

The earth becomes a great deportation camp, where men await celestial redemption. Which God-the-Father alone, in his anger and jealousy, may initiate and bring about. Manifesting his wishes to the posterity of that first couple. Gathering a people of children. An elect, who are more or less obedient, more or less faithful, more or less rewarded or punished. Who till the ground, build a world, establish private properties. Genealogy of patriarchs who are guardians to a Word transmitted to male heirs alone.

The course followed in the Bible testifies that God still shows himself in person to Abraham and Sarah, Jacob, Moses. First a meeting of persons, through the senses. God still allows himself to be heard, seen, touched. The trace of God's passage is marked in the man's body and in his change of name (are men subjected in the Covenant to what happens to women in marriage?). The demands between God and men are still explicitly reciprocal. Orders are still discussed, even argued over. God is not the All-Powerful who has vanished into his Heaven and dispenses his seeds of truth from the heights of that distance. He is there—physically, sensorially, cosmically.

But this presence that is so real and material will be transmuted into a law inscribed in stone. The Word of God is heard, is venerated in the form of writing. He is withheld from immediate contact, given over to commentators and translators. The last time that He appears, he allows himself to be seen only from the back, to a man standing in the crack of a rock. His face—and his sex?—is no longer to be seen in its Glory. It is definitively Other. While the man Moses, that figuration of body and sex that are still incarnate and mortal, takes refuge in a natural crevice.

Moment of ecstasy of the divine in relation to the human. Historic inscription of the myth of the lost paradise. Intrabiblical constitution of the doubling and the splitting of man between his earthly life and his God. Illustration of his two bodies, his two sexes, his two languages, perhaps? Aspiration and creation of a Transcendent that is no longer manifest here and now, but is deciphered from signs carved into stone. Interpretation of the Word that at times contradicts the one that commands through the mouth of the prophets.

Then begin the wars between the peoples, between chiefs of nations, between scribes or priests, between men—as to who possesses the true God. His is also an armed presence. Made real and attested to by military command and triumph. Fights to the death about who shall take over the signs, the insignia, of belonging to the God of gods. Whose will, inscribed upon tablets, is sealed up to protect it from the tangible approach of simple mortals.

But God himself is divided between his law as inscribed in mineral and a cloud that accompanies and makes a sign to his people— divided between the most immutably fixed and the most lightly airy, between the least and the most porous. . . And, inside the ark, he is to be found in the place that is left empty between. In the between that has yet to occur. In the still possible between. Is this a memorial to a nearness that dwells and remains in the air? That occurs sometimes, like a trembling of the space between cherubim. A medium in which his tangible advent is sensed, set up, prepared. Guarded, safeguarded by angels, between their wings.

Meanwhile men are killing each other and draping themselves in the garments of glory. How will God escape these armed conflicts? How will the Chosen People lose their monopoly on his power? How will the assurance that they possess his glory be taken from them? Their temple, their sanctuary, their trappings, their cult will be emptied of the presence of God. Destroyed, and by fire. God, who avenges idolatry. Using his enemies against his friends, foreigners against the faithful. Where has God gone to? Who may still claim to be his child? To be the guardian of his Presence? Neither he who believed he had taken possession of it nor he who had annihilated it in his temple. Who?

He returns in an unexpected place and in an unexpected guise. In the womb of a woman. Is she the only one left who still has some understanding of the divine? Who still listens silently and gives new flesh to what she perceived in those messages that other people cannot perceive? Can she alone feel the music of the air trembling between the wings of the angels, and make or remake a body from it?

Without that virgin's sensitivity—that ability to sense and open up to the most delicate vibration—how could he whom we call Jesus of Nazareth be born? And if God, in the beginning, "created" man and woman, could the unheard of and scandalous part about Jesus of Nazareth's coming into the world be that he issues forth from a woman? A virgin-mother would give God back to God. A tardy, and quickly neglected, recognition of woman's share in creation? Cocreation of a divine nature? The presence that had been buried and paralyzed in the text of the law is made flesh once more in the body of a woman, guardian of the spirit of the divine life.

God's presence reappears in a different way. Having returned to earth, conceived and born by an attentive love, he manifests the miraculous power of that love. Never a slave to the law, making every text contradict itself, elusive in any formula adopted, escaping any prevailing cult, any idolatry. Living in "an infantilism that has receded into the spiritual," a holy innocence (Nietzsche, *Antichrist,* sec. 32), "a state of the heart" that is the "kingdom of heaven," a "general feeling of transfiguration of every thing (beatitude)," to which "the entry" is designated by the word "Son" and that "the word father expresses" in his "perfection," his "eternity" (*idem,* sec. 34), manifesting the "kingdom of God" as something that can take place here and now, with no nostalgia for yesterday, no expectation for some day in the future, and more importantly for some day after death *(ibid.).* The Christ would incarnate "a new way of life and *not* a new faith," a certain "practice" of life that knows not sin, opposition, distance, judgment, penitence, all ways to say "no" to the love of what is (*idem,* sec. 33).

Does this necessarily mean 'the sequel of degeneracy; the case of a delayed puberty, which the organism does not bring to term" (*idem,* sec. 32). Perhaps. But Dionysos also remains a child. Is more commonly represented as the newborn who is watched over, rocked, surrounded by mothers—nurses and mistresses. When he dies he looks like a little boy not an adult. Clearly he does not, in himself, overcome the contradictions. But rather draws them to their paroxysm—murderer and victim, rent and rending. Torn limb from limb between the abysses on high and on low, between Olympus and the depths of the sea. Already divine, still human. Never in control of the passion of opposites. Not even in his ressurections.

The Christ, apparently, resolves things. The "Good News" is exactly this: love can reconcile antagonisms. Metabolize them without being torn apart. But the gospels, the Christian institutions and dogmas have erased all trace of the practice of his *eros*. Unless one thinks—or believes?—that fleshly relations were in him suspended, shunned: "the instinctive love of reality: consequence of an extreme sensitivity to pain and stimulus, that cannot bear to be 'touched' because it feels any contact too deeply"? (*idem*, sec. 30).

Was he like that? Or has tradition made him like that? The place of his loves is rendered as virgin, or childlike, or adolescent. Must the Christic redemption mean that the advent of the divine has never taken place in the incarnation of a loving relation with the other? Must this messenger of life neglect or refuse the most elementary realities? Must he be a timid or morbid adolescent, too paralyzed to realize his desires, always attentive to his Father's edicts, executing the Father's wishes even to the point of accepting the passion and the Father's desertion as the price of such fidelity. And then death. . . And without posterity. Except symbolic posterity. But which?

Who interpreted him in this way? Who abominated the body so much that he glorified the son of man for being abstinent, castrated? And why was it necessary for Christ to die and rise again in order for men to believe he was God? Why could his presence in the flesh not be perceived as divine? The heavenly kingdom is at hand only when the flesh has been stripped away. God does not exist without infinite distance and exile. Being beyond all experience in the world of the senses. Which is forgotten at the outset?

But where does the man who conceives of God in this way find the grounds for his conception? From whom does he take the matter to frame it with? And if he produces it out of himself, what kind of contorsions does he have to engage in if he has to return back to himself from On High—One, unique, perfect, Immutable. . . What does he fail to understand about that part of him that comes back in this way and to which he attaches his becoming? Begging it/himself to enter into eternity whereas he is already dead to time, immune to change. What refusal, rejection, hatred of the other—and of the self as always other—intervene in this adoration? Imperceptibly things freeze up, move apart, making any passage or sharing between impossible. An All Powerful who is forever distant is erected because no one understands what enters into his constitution, perhaps?

Inaccessible God. Separated by a horizon-veil that hides him away from the perception of mortals. From experience by the senses. Unless the experience be "internal" and solitary? Possible relapse into an illusion that paralyzes all access to the other, suspends all motions between, withholds the movement of attuning oneself with. Place of a mourning that refuses to make a return to the moment when "God" was adored for the first time. Setting its aim or its object infinitely at one remove, in space and time. With the most loving—or the risk—staged as a sleep or a dream?

God—who makes up for word and flesh being torn apart. Who maintains, as a result of his "attributes" the gap between, the impossible reconciliation. Word of the Father that comforts impotence but makes a law and sets power up in the name of that law. Is this an order that has come down from Heaven as suprasensory palliative to all that still remains silent in the flesh, remains "in limbo"? Awaiting the parousia, perhaps? Although the Messiah has come? How is this to be understood?

Whether on the far side or the near side of any Christian tradition, does not the Christ—second son of Adam, innocent son of the Father—manifest the tragic destiny of love and desire imprisoned in a single body? Seeking to express themselves through all the senses, and in the end being crucified—on the level of touch. That mediatory sense par excellence. The sense that, most darkly, overcomes the distances between, the enclosure within distinct forms, the borders dividing up territories and private estates. Sense that gets through the walls of the tomb where the flesh lies captive. Sepulcher of stone, ice, dream or letter—an impermeable skin that shuts each man up within the boundaries of his death. A necessary perspective, no doubt, but one which, again and again, could open up to permit an ever renewed becoming. In which the limit of each man was respected but which allowed access to something more than individuation, to an exchange with the other in his/her difference.

"The very word *Christianity* rests upon a misunderstanding; basically there has only been one Christian, and he died on the cross. The "Gospel" *died* on the cross." (*Antichrist*, sec. 39). The "Good

News" was crucified as it was heralded. In order to fulfill the will of the Father? or because it could not be received. Do these two interpretations still and forever amount to the same thing?

What is the meaning of the event of the incarnation which follows upon the metamorphoses of God's presence recorded in the Jewish tradition, and the decadent triumph of measured restraint in Greek culture? What does it mean that the word is made flesh? Why does its prophecy have such a wide influence? And, despite all the well-known horrors and repressions, how do we account for all the works of art which that prophecy gave rise to? What energy let them root and flourish, through the centuries, as places where the divine lives and breathes? Can the legalism, the sentence, even the ressentiment of Christianity claim and take credit for the enthusiasm and exuberance of that creation? Or does the inspiration blossom despite and in opposition to all moralizing? And can that creative strength be reduced to the power of the love between son and father, that matrix for idealism, with the virgin-mother as its sensory-substrate? Are the desire and the sharing of the flesh not at work here? Don't they sing here? Don't they paint? Sculpt? Speak? In a language that of course goes beyond and stops short of any grammar of reason. Cryptic, or mystic, in its language. In accordance with sketches, shapes, a graphic system, a symbolism that has no preestablished framework. Something always, and at each opportunity, heretical in the eyes of orthodoxy. Which condemns anything that does not obey the norm.

And therefore condemns Christ? Figure of love transgressing the limits of written history, law, letter. Reopening and circulating the flow of life despite all that captures, encloses, restrains life—tomb, mask, signs. But must he who breaks the seal of the letter suffer the penalty in return? Crucified for a word? Like a word? Or a symbol? Whereas—or just because—the use he made of it was intended as a parabolic approach. Never definitive, never completed. Never definitively plumbed in its meaning, perhaps, never wholly decoded? Revelation of something still to come that is looking for its figure? Its covenant?

Is this store any more understood or accepted, in its openness, than nature or women might have been for Dionysos? Wasn't it necessary to strike to find life there and make it spring forth? To kill, so that the women might rise from the dead? As if that movement of bloom and decay, of flowering and dying back, of death and resurrection were not already natural? And as if a recreation of a divine

179

nature were necessary. A doubling of a movement already in place. A kind of recapitulation, of mimicry occurring in Heaven, that supposedly gives rise to everything. Or gives rise to everything again?

For example the child-god. Who is not even procreated in the womb of a mortal woman. Son of the Father conceived by the Word in a virgin. Immaculate in his conception, as she in hers.

Which can be understood in different ways. As a myth of extraordinary birth. As, and through some form of reversal, the symbol of an interdict laid upon the flesh. Or as the fact that the woman-mother of this advent was innocent of the laws, specifically the laws of love. Had no knowledge of the imperatives of desire. Was outside any conjugal institution. Was not marked by the language of a father-husband. A virgin in the eyes of the traditional order. Receptive to the whole of the world—to all that is forgotten and all that is to come. Listening to the breath of the spirit? That overcomes walls dividing property. Seed that goes beyond and stops short of any word ever written, any land ever conquered. That might perhaps give birth to a new figure of history? Arriving from beyond the sky, by the mediation of an angel?

Strange genealogy. . . Who is who in this Holy Family? Not one name is in its place. The father isn't really the father. The mother? Equally not, by the usual standards. The son? Will not perpetuate either the name or the patrimony, in a certain sense. He is always known either by a first name or a given name, and he will be judged, condemned, crucified for a question of designation! As for worldly goods, what does he have to bequeath, except his own flesh?

The patriarchal machine locks, clogs. Is suspended from Heaven. To and from which climbs a certain mystery, a certain disorder that is attributed to the spirit. In his role as absolute guarantee, the eternal Father would cover everything there is from his Height.

What exactly? The love of the son for him? That for sure, and in a never absolute perfection: "Christ is the end. And doubtless another nature still, but he perfects that which is lacking in the others, so that the presence of the Divine Ones might be total."* (Holderlin, *Hymns*, "The Unique," third version). The Christ would supposedly complete the realization of the figure of a paternal Omnipotence.

---

*Hölderlin, *Poèmes (Gedichte)*, traduction et préface de Geneviève Bianqui (Paris: Aubier, Editions Montaigne, 1943), pp. 404–405.—Tr.

End of the struggle between the old and the new gods. The divinatory power of the ancestress and of the maternal and female divinities who still threaten man's destiny would be overcome once and for all? Hellenic and Jewish cultures would unite to give birth to this ideal: the triumph of one single God? Of a Transcendence that can be attained only through death and resurrection?

Is he not of "another nature still"? Near at hand, who loved the Christ? Tradition is largely silent here. Must we interpret the Christic symbol as consecration of a love that is carried over after death, or as a quest for some incredible nearness in life? A nearness revealed by the effect it has, read in certain gestures or words. Eluding a single way of speaking or showing? Always and still prophetic.

Was he really untouchable? His miracles are usually based on touch. Even his words aim to touch rather than to prove or convince. His teaching is almost always contradictory, and converts or heals by touching. A touch that is not a violent attack, like that of Dionysos. That does not strike from afar—like Zeus or Apollo, or even Dionysos. That is respectful of bodily space, of sensual space, of openings in the skin. Each one remains himself, these and those get close, meet, touch one another. Sometimes by a miracle in the moment, sometimes by a parable. So that history may be understood without understanding—may sprout where no one hears. Achieved from the depths of a flesh that sometimes needs time. Does not bear rape. But remains impassive to the letter enveloping or masking the message. The letter does not touch, it is too explicit and too cryptic. It remains outside the body. Is not, is no longer, made flesh. Kills or dies. Forbids crime, of course, but is not life-giving. A skin that has been shed, abandoned, or else so jealously closed over itself that nothing can get through it.

The word made flesh in Mary might mean—might it not?—the advent of a divine one who does not burst in violently, like the god of Greek desire, does not simply rule the world from a heaven of dreams, and does not remain closed in a text of law either. Neither bursts on the scene nor slips suddenly away, does not act to defer the possibility that the presence will occur. The god does not brutally enter a body, only to throw it off at once, leaving it to madness and the death of a boundless passion. He does not hide behind an unending series of appearances that ease the pain of living by giving mortals a chance to gaze upon an alien perfection. He is not made known only through writing.

He is made flesh. Continues on in the flesh. Closes with and is close to himself, from within a living body. That can be affected by *pathos*—his own and that of others.

This aspect of Christ is still to be discovered. After the unveiling of the figures who made him into the God of ontotheology: master of truth or of morality. Masks that are still made to the pattern of an idolatrous fiction. God constituted by the standard of men's desires at compromising periods of history. Man is called to yield, to grovel, to give the self up so as to find it again within an All-Powerfulness that has been forged according to an overabundance of passions paralyzed by fear, obedience, and ressentiment. Father created by man in his idea or his image. According to a model that today is doomed to decline.

But perhaps a certain kind of divine has never taken place, even though it has been heralded. One that has never been mummified in a single name, face, or figure. A single letter or law that has already been fetishized. One that is coming. That comes near in the flesh with a certain restraint. Not eternally deferring its coming, but expecting the expectation of the other before it presents itself, offers itself. Penetrates the other lovingly. Dwells in the other, without taking over. And receives, in return.

For this god-man does not exist in a triumphant self-sufficiency. Always he is in society, in company, loved, helped. Living in a society of living people, from which he does not emerge as a solitary man. Sharing needs and desires with mortals. Leading them, no doubt, to the limit of their *pathein*. Trying, nonetheless, to observe some restraint as measured by the limits of a body. This god eats, drinks, sleeps, goes off alone and comes back, speaks or is silent, listens and answers, walks or stops, lives secretly or in the open, goes into hiding or comes forth publicly, loves and suffers desertion and betrayal, has close friends, political enemies, judges, admirers . . . What distinguishes him from the most mortal of mortals? Apparently nothing. Except that he preserves within himself the divine dimension? What is there to say about this? What does he say about it? He sees the divine dimension. It determines everything he does or doesn't do and say. It is impossible to pin down. Impossible to lay a hand on, yet always present. Breathed into the core of his flesh. Inapparent, yet feeding all that appears. Shining through each of his acts.

The divine cannot be located as such, imagined or conceived of as such, taken over as such—might that not be its prophecy? It refreshes anyone who receives it and is inspired by it. It lives everywhere and nowhere. Has no fixed abode. It leaves the temple for nature, the house for the city, the lake for the desert, contemplation for action, restraint for passion ... Moves about and keeps still. Keeps watch, while abandoning any fixed fidelity. Passing through any fixed framework, any body of law, any edict promulgated. Moving round endlessly through everything and yet, at the same time, tenaciously following a trail from which it never deviates. Accomplishing the will of an Other? Incarnating transcendence? Not to be reduced to that secular paradigm—a "son" obeying a "Father." But a man who unites in himself all dimensions. Even including the cross? Crossroads that pulled him up short. Where he was standing endlessly. Might the fact that he was sacrificed on the cross mean, among other things, that unless the human gives up certain directions it always finds itself at a crossroads? He had no wish to be nailed upon the cross and held in that position. The effigy was not his place of choice. Anyone who wants to fix him on the cross forgets all the rest. Chooses to find him where he did not choose to be. Paralysis was never his rhythm. Even when dead, he rose again. Is resurrected, moves out of the walls of the tomb, reappears in the body, ascends into heaven, comes back in the spirit. Lives, lives again, lives on through it all.

Is this the way with love that has overcome hatred? When a body becomes a barrier that cannot be crossed, something closed off inside its own skin, or place, or world, isn't this the work of hatred? Doesn't Christianity forget this? Remain the prisoner of hate? With its Distance and Difference, its Heaven and its hell, its good men and sinners, its last judgment, its morality of retribution and punishment, its inquisitions and persecutions, its charity...

Certainly, Christianity is thus. What about Christ? Is his reluctance to show loving passion an effect or an evaluation of hatred? And the times he goes off to be alone? And the veil over the fulfillment of his desires? And his cries when he is forsaken? And his death? Active vigilance to guard against the irruptions of hatred, passive consent to its violence when no avoidance is possible, except by denying oneself.

Seen in this light, his life would herald an age of love, with the crucifixion marking the testing and failure of that age. At that moment in history? Hatred triumphs. Has the upper hand. The man who did not wish to enter violently into the body of the other dies pierced with thorns, nails, lance. The environment created by the incarnation yields to the play of hostile forces. Does it succumb to the reaction secreted by any powerful establishment? Any world built up simply by a will for power?

But perhaps it was necessary that hatred, in all its horror, should figure in that life, just so that love should not look like childish innocence—candidly or morbidly ignorant of passion and excess. For childhood is not lacking in cruelty. Ought Dionysos, while still in the cradle, appear to be the vigorous double of a degenerate Christ-child? Dionysos/the Crucified One, a different pairing, a doubling other than the one illustrated by Apollo/Dionysos? With the Crucified One playing the role of a twin who is easily overcome by Dionysos, whose wrestling match with his other twin, Apollo, would continue to lead the game.

The Christ, as fragile little brother of the god of Greek desire, would seem a part of the Apollonian configuration as a result of the beauty of his gestures, his transfiguration, his resurrection, even through the sublimity of his death. Christ—the great artist? Seen this way, what splendor to die in the flower of life! A masterly way to cover over decline! Dying becomes desirable. The pain of sacrifice stirs the senses, blurs the mind. Gives comfort for the pain of living. Happy oblivion—of suffering and laughter. The horror of immolation is changed into ecstatic contemplation. The passion of the crucifixion spreads like a celestial horizon. Murder becomes rapture in which blood ransoms past and future. A tableau surpassing any other show. Nailing the gesture. Paralyzing the sculptor himself. Flooding the eye in shadow. Inimitable in the perfection of its model. What God can do better than offer himself thus to the very heights of rending love?

Creation of a divine nature. Analogous, perhaps, to the process of being torn apart, lacerated, shredded, killed, to which the primitive cosmic unity was subject. That henceforth is veiled by the spectacle of the crucified Christ. A tragedy that is indeed cruelly optimistic, logical, serene—redemptive. A *pathein* that has submitted to the order and the will of the Father. Reaching the Absolute in order to lead and shepherd a people back to their God. A deed done once and for all.

What remains, perhaps, is faith in him. Becoming him. The Idea of ideas would have been incarnated in one "only son," who is henceforward offered for imitation. The mirror would have come down from Heaven. Coming near to us. The artistic phenomenon par excellence. That would proscribe art insofar as it had already perfected art.

Did the crucified one retain from Apollo the heart pierced by a lance? The trace of a wound remaining in the lonely stance of the man-god. The mark that he always produces himself out of a woman-mother. "Wound" in which he finds his first and last inspiration. Of Dionysos, he would be nothing but the mask made man, the painted figure. The tunic? that is torn into pieces. The bread and wine in which he gives himself as food.

But isn't it possible that in him, two skins have been mixed up? The skin called veil of appearance that imperceptibly covers over the Truth, and the skin that marks the boundaries of a living being? The god of love would have to overcome two deaths: death by being buried in a personage or a Person, and death by being imprisoned in a body. With his sepulcher repeating, so as to pass beyond, the ways he is closed into something already dead. It was necessary for Christ to be made into a corpse in order for the resurrection to reveal that, in him, the flesh overcomes the walls of tombs. Necessary double resurrection. And only predicted in Jesus Christ? Never fulfilled, according to tradition.

For tradition refuses to show Christ in the nakedness of his incarnation. But always sets him in the pattern of Goodness only. Fails to free his message from the mask of Truth. Wraps it up once again by reassigning it to the Idea that paralyzes all loving becoming. Submits it to a law that forbids the *pathein* of the flesh. Which in turn is left to the province of art. Is artistically effigied, but never acted upon or suffered in daily life.

Might the effect of the Christian message depend upon the degree to which it is being constantly repressed? With the "Good News" of the incarnation being constantly misunderstood, censored, rejected, forgotten. Always aiming to be overcome in the anticipation of a resurrection after death, in the hope of another life? A sur-vival, an over-life? Closing off the space-time in which the divine can occur within and between bodies? That prophecy would be eliminated so as to set up yet another "suprasensory" God. Alien to the world. Infinitely, loftily distant from us here and now. Unattainable in this life. Our flesh, forever corrupt. Our body, forever incapable of love and desire. Always in excess or in default. Always in agony.

What mania for All-Powerfulness inspires such a conception of man and the world? By projecting that mania into Christ, isn't he made into the least lovable of all gods? Putting in him everything a Christian tradition aimed to get rid of? But didn't that tradition also keep in some kind of insistent latency everything in the gospel that it refused? The mystery of an incarnate divine. Split apart, by the priests of ressentiment, between Heaven and hell. Sublime and unattainable distance of a God-Father, intolerable brazier to which anyone comes who does not overcome passion. Alternations beyond rhyme or reason are expelled from a disaffected world. A place of exile.

Incarnation—into exile, or out of it? No more land, temple, people charged with some special privilege, just a body. The most difficult operation? Any detour is valuable if it can hide this revelation: the divine wishes to dwell in the flesh. The most glaring part of the rejection of this advent is—to lay a ban upon the flesh itself. To set Christ up as an idol of incarnation? By neglecting the simplest—or is it the most difficult?—part of his message.

Is there still reinterpretation to be done short of or beyond all ontotheology? All theophany that has already been revealed? Then, perhaps, discover their masks.

The perfection of love between son and Father, with its completion in a Trinity, schematizes to an extreme degree the relationship underpinning the foundation and development of the ontotheology. In which Christ is resolved or not resolved. Is enclosed or runs loose. Dies as God, or is at last at hand.

If this figure of love must continue to be unique, remaining eternally captive to the lure of a (male) Same, what use is it to dig it up today? Has it not already had any effect it is going to have? Is it not the pattern for the mask that completes, to the point of inappearance, man's identity with himself? The dream of becoming the self without contradictions, of reabsorbing into the self all things opposed and different, of subsuming under the self the transcendent of oneself. Of one day finally being divinely the self.

There would be nothing there but love of self. Therefore, no love? Christ would not be Dionysos's latterday twin, but a monster of egoism, a Narcissus who ends up reabsorbing his highest idea or ideal into Himself.

What would be surprising in this? The lack of conflict with the Father. Who is, henceforward, once and for all, in heaven. Never here anymore. Model withheld from mortal gaze. Perfection men would have to strive for without being able to evaluate it with their senses. Imitating the "son." Walking, believing in the Word, toward a single God. In several persons, several masks, several manifestations, several exemplars that we might, today, decode?

But why a god of love, given the effects and the illustrations we know about? Unless exclusive love of the Father is only a partial translation of his message? Unless the nonconflictual fulfillment of this relationship to the Other left a place for the other? The life of Christ, perhaps, cannot be reduced to the *pathein* of the Father's will. It would open the way for the transcendence of the other that has always been covered over by the Father-son paradigm. Whereby love, desire, creation within the same, sparing Distance or Difference all the more because, in some measure, they do not exist. The abyss opens up because they are not revealed.

Nietzsche—perhaps—has experienced and shown what is the result of infinite distance reabsorbed into the (male) same, shown the difference that remains without a face or countenance. By wishing to overcome everything, he plunges into the shadows—lit up and with no perspective. As he becomes the whole of the world's time, he has no point of view left that would allow him to see. Ariadne, or Diotima, or . . . no longer even return his mask or his gaze. He is mask and blinded eye. Once his creation is realized, he lives it. And nothing else. There is no other that might allow him to continue to make himself flesh. No other to set the limits of his corporeal identity with and for him, putting his latest thought into the background so a new one can be born.

The sacrifice he makes to the Idea is inscribed in this—that he preferred the Idea to an ever provisional openness to a female other. That he refused to break the mirror of the (male) same, and over and over again demanded that the other be his double. To the point of willing to become that female other. Despite all physiology, all incarnation. Hermit, tightrope walker or bird, forgetful of her who gave him birth and company and norishment, he soars up, leaving everything below him or inside him, and the chasm becomes bottomless.

And what would Ariadne's or Diotima's or anyone else's "yes" have changed? Nothing in his thinking. Unless a woman refuses to be woman, at least according to his definition. Asserts her difference. Therefore not Ariadne, that abyss for his passion. An Apollonian partner? Setting him up once and for all as a work of art? Paralyzing him in his Dionysian becoming. Insoluble fate. Sensing the impotence to come, Nietzsche declares he is the crucified one. And is crucified. But by himself.

Either Christ overwhelms that tragedy, or Nietzsche overcomes Christ. By repeating-parodying the Christian advent, what does he unmask in his gesture? That Christ is nothing that still deserves to live, or that his age is yet to come?

This reevaluation is possible only if he goes beyond the Father-son relationship. If he announces—beyond Christianity?—that only through difference can the incarnation unfold without murderous or suicidal passion. Rhythm and measure of a female other that, endlessly, undoes the autological circle of discourse, thwarts the eternal return of the same, opens up every horizon through the affirmation of another point of view whose fulfillment can never be predicted. That is always dangerous? A gay science of the incarnation?

To which the female side would, up to now, have served only as a protective shadow. Setting up perspective, through a kind of resistance to the already-existing light. Never desired or loved for herself, but forming a screen for the dazzling and blinding collusion of Father-son. A reminder that man comes from the earth-mother, that he returns to her, and that at each step a shadow walks by his side.

The will to leap over that shadow or to lend her light that does not suit her, amounts once again to belittling her as other. To entering into autistic madness. Making oneself the only God. If that Idol means the whole of love, then love always amounts to a murder—the murder of the other. Which remains a crime whether or not it is sublimated under a capital letter as Difference or Distance. Which consecrates crime. Glorifying it despite, or within, the sacrifice once more subsumed into the same. Thanks to the passion of the "son" perhaps?

But doesn't his cross mark the impossibility of any relationship to the other? The love that ebbs backward into sameness, unable to either give or receive. To exchange or pattern oneself among different bodies, words, flesh? The lonely fading away of a gesture that was motivated also by the other? And plunges down into the abyss, rather than surrender.

Is the Crucified One the sign of such an economy of love and desire? To interpret him therefore means "go beyond" if possible without return. Not be satisfied with such a love. Leave it to the men of ressentiment, and try to create another world.

And if it is another love that he heralds, then deliver him from his masks of death, and set him once more in his flesh. While trying not to kill him, one more time, with hatred, albeit veiled, of the law. A law that congeals an ideal figure of love. Sending that figure back to some hideaway in the Infinite does not wipe out its unique qualities. The idol keeps from falling. Never allows itself to be perceived as such. Remains, nonetheless, the only place of cathexis. Of aspiration that exhausts the whole of the breath. All the more alluring because eternally deferring the encounter. Promise of a something beyond death, in which life would leave the tombs behind at last, and enter into its glory.

Men perhaps? know no other way to the divine, even if some sense it nostalgically. The immediate coming of the god brings them nothing but madness or paralysis. And as they constantly back away from such a sudden experience of the divine, they measure up only to themselves, even in regard to their God. Measuring out the path that marks the boundary of their world. From hell to Heaven.

But this way they always stay within their limits. Anything set on either side of those limits is defined by them. Whether they know it or not, wish it or not. They include in this circle the other of nature, by mimicking her, perfecting her artistically, that is certain. They operate by taking things over. God, the name given to the abyss in which nature is established and prevented from revealing herself. Only the world they create exists. Visible and invisible offered or withheld according to their will alone, their gaze alone. In which any nativity would germinate, to which it would return. In nativity man would still and always see only himself. Giving pictures and names only to his creatures.

A love that knows no other. Except as a foundation or shadow for an idea of self that never puts itself on display in a simple way. The other would be merely one of the masks of the same. One figure, one face, one sort of presence accompanying man's becoming. Sometimes tragic, sometimes serenely contemplative. Now dark with shadows, now beaming forth an excess of light as it waits to be disposed in new landscapes. In hollow, in lack or in excess, man would perceive and receive nothing except from his own eye.

The other has yet to enlighten him. To tell him something. Even to appear to him in her irreducibility. The impossibility of overcoming her. And if, to the whole of himself, he says "yes" and also asks her to say "yes" again, did it ever occur to him to say "yes" to her? Did he ever open himself to that other world? For him it doesn't even exist. So who speaks of love, to the other, without having even begun to say "yes"?

☆

To "go beyond." Or decode the Christic symbol beyond any traditional morality. To read, in it, the fruit of the covenant between word and nature, between *logos* and *cosmos*. A marriage that has never been consummated and that the spirit, in Mary, would renew?

The spirit? Not, this time, the product of the love between Father and son, but the universe already made flesh or capable of becoming flesh, and remaining in excess to the existing world.

Grace that speaks silently through and beyond the word?